2009

Dearest Alison

On the occasion of your 50th birthday, may I say how delighted I am to have known you all these years. As we all head to the Autumn of our lives, I'd just like to say, it's time to travel!

With love always

Ruth

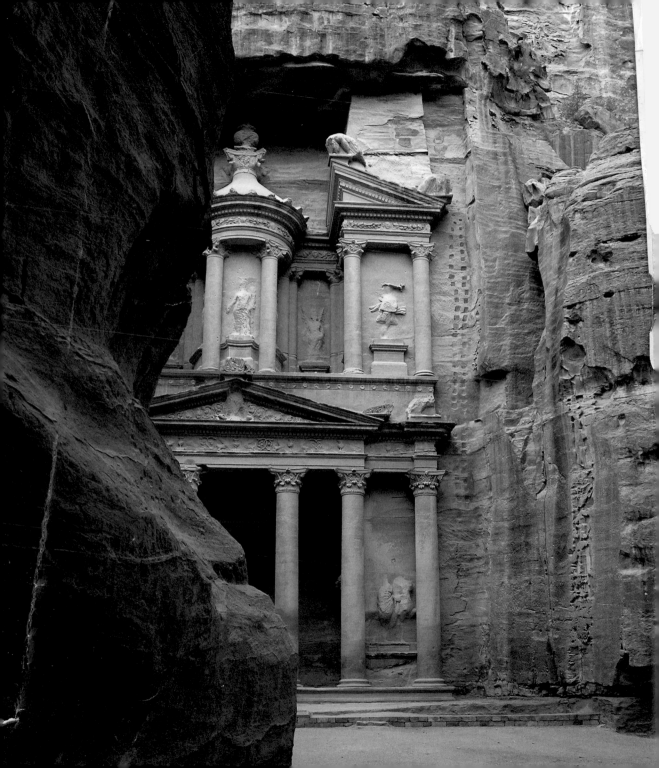

THE BIG SHORT BREAK

THE BIG SHORT BREAK

MINIMUM TIME » MAXIMUM EXPERIENCE

RONALD ASPREY

©2007 Original Publishing

First published in the United Kingdom in 2007 by
Original Publishing, 1B The Village, 101 Amies Street
London SW11 2JW

thebigshortbreak.co.uk

Designed and typeset by Inaria
inaria-design.com

Edited by Tom Barber
Project managed by Emily Morris
Cover image by Chris Simpson; Namib Desert, Namibia
Printed in the United Kingdom by CTD

Although every effort has been made to ensure
that the information contained within this book is
as up-to-date and accurate as possible at the
time of going to press, some details are liable
to change.

British Library Cataloguing-in-Publication Data.
A catalogue record for this book is available from
the British Library.

ISBN 978-0-9555935-0-5

THE BIG SHORT BREAK

CONTENTS

THE BIG IDEA » It goes without saying in this hectic modern world of ours that holidays are valuable. Knowing how to make the best use of your days off (and we in Britain get fewer than most) is therefore crucial, which is where this book should prove an invaluable resource.

So what exactly is a Big Short Break? It's not quite time travel, but until that becomes a reality, think of it as the ideal solution to combining a busy work life with, well, a life. A A Gill calls it an 'espresso break' – a short, sharp hit of travel that provides a change of scene and mental refreshment. The simple fact is that taking regular breaks is good for you. A shorter break also means you're not faced with a mountainous backlog of work on your return, which can soon leave you feeling decaffeinated again.

And while air travel is a significant contributor to CO_2 emissions, the team behind this book (see page 344) is committed to reducing the negative impact of flying through its partnership with carbon offset organisation Climate Care, and also supports responsible tourism projects specific to the destinations within these pages.

At least a third of people in the UK do not use their full annual holiday allowance. With this collection of Big Short Breaks that are short on time but long on experience, you can now make every day count.

RONALD ASPREY
2007

THE BIG
SHORT BREAK
MINIMUM TIME »
MAXIMUM
EXPERIENCE

THE BIG SHORT BREAK » This portfolio of Big Short Breaks is brought to you by award-winning travel company Original Travel. The trips are designed to offer as broad a range of destinations and experiences as possible, while remaining feasible within the confines of a short break. For the most part, the trips are experience-led, with the emphasis on the destination and the activities available – though we have also included our favourite hotels in each case, one or two of which are destinations in their own right.

The Big Short Breaks are arranged by season according to what we consider the optimum time of year to travel. They are further divided into six categories: Safaris, Escapes, Adventures, Skiing, Cities and Kids – the latter for those trips particularly well-suited to families. From dog-sledding in Lapland to a safari in the Serengeti, and from exploring the sights of Istanbul to chilling on a Mediterranean beach, each trip featured on these pages has been independently chosen, and personally vetted, by the Original Travel team. With the exception of Havana (which is simply too cool a destination to leave out) every destination can be reached within reasonable flying time from the UK or via an overnight flight. After all, on a short break, you want to hit the ground running. The suggested itineraries for each trip are just a guideline – every Big Short Break can be tailored as required.

We hope you will be inspired by this book – you'll be surprised at what you can do in just a few short days. Original Travel, Original Thinking.

ORIGINAL TRAVEL

KEY TO ICONS FOR EACH
BIG SHORT BREAK

✈ LENGTH OF INTERNATIONAL & LOCAL FLIGHTS,
INDICATED TO THE NEAREST HALF HOUR

🧳 NUMBER OF DAYS AWAY & MINIMUM NUMBER OF DAYS
REQUIRED OFF WORK (ASSUMING NO BANK HOLIDAY)

☀ AVERAGE MAXIMUM & MINIMUM MONTHLY
TEMPERATURES FOR EACH SEASON

* Flight times are based on international
flights taken from the UK and do
not include onward transfers.

** Prices are per person, based on
two people sharing and inclusive of
flights in economy class, transfers and
accommodation. Subject to availability.
Prices are correct at time of going
to press.

01
SPRING

EXPERIENCE THIS »

RACE OVER THE SNOW AT 60MPH THROUGH
EERIE, MISTY VALLEYS AND SPECTACULAR GLACIAL
SCENERY, KNOWING THAT YOU'RE MOST LIKELY
BEING WATCHED BY POLAR BEARS.

SVALBARD

SVALBARD ARCTIC
ADVENTURE

Spitsbergen

Longyearbyen

MUST SEE Glaciers
calving straight into the
icy sea at Tempelfjorden
» If you're lucky, the
Northern Lights » The
effects of global warming,
which is altering the
climate of the polar
regions more rapidly
than anywhere else

MUST DO Track polar
bears on a snowmobile
safari » Drive your own
team of huskies » Explore
the inside of a glacier
RESTAURANTS/BARS
The popular Barentz
Pub will serve you the
northernmost pint on
planet Earth SOUVENIRS

Stunning images from
local photographer
Herta Grondal BOOK
TO PACK Arctic Dreams:
Imagination and Desire
in a Northern Landscape
by Barry Lopez DON'T
FORGET... Slippers... it's
customary in Svalbard
to take off your shoes

before entering a home
and this goes for hotels
and restaurants too.
Pack slippers if you don't
want to walk around
in your socks

PRICE ■■■□□

BEST FOR… WOULD-BE POLAR EXPLORERS » Where? Not many people have heard of Svalbard, though some might recall it as one of the settings for Philip Pullman's *His Dark Materials* books. First discovered by Vikings in the 12th century, Svalbard – which means 'cold coast' in old Norse – is a remote archipelago in the Arctic Ocean, north of Norway. To give you an idea of just how far north we're talking, Oslo is almost as close to Africa as it is to Svalbard. It is so remote that the Norwegians are building a 'doomsday vault' there which will contain a seed bank for all the world's most important crop plants, designed to preserve them in the event of a global catastrophe. Once a departure point for polar explorers like Roald Amundsen, Svalbard is clearly not your typical weekend destination, but for adventurous souls it offers a surprisingly accessible opportunity to experience untouched Arctic wilderness. Dog-sledding across Spitsbergen, the main island, takes you through frozen landscapes of glaciers, mountains and fjords full of blue icebergs – think the Scottish Highlands during an ice age – or you can go in search of polar bears, which hunt for seal on the pack-ice. Other wildlife includes reindeer, walrus and ptarmigan (snow grouse). Spring is a good time to travel to Svalbard, with a permanent orange twilight glow giving way to midnight sun by late April.

TAKE ME THERE
thebigshortbreak.co.uk
+44 (0)20 7978 7333

SVALBARD ARCTIC ADVENTURE

✈ 2 HRS FROM UK
3 HRS TRANSFER

🧳 4 DAYS
2 DAYS OFF WORK

☀ MAR 15°/-9°; APR -12°/-5°
MAY -5°/-1°

DAY 1 Evening flight to Oslo, connecting to Longyearbyen, the main settlement of Svalbard » If you're travelling in late April or May it will still be light when you land at around 0100 » Overnight in Longyearbyen

DAY 2 Morning dog-sledding trip: meet and harness your husky team for the 3-hour sled ride up the local valley » Afternoon at leisure to explore Longyearbyen

DAY 3 Early start for full-day snowmobile safari, tracking polar bears on the east coast » Drive on the frozen ocean up to the foot of glaciers, past vivid blue icebergs and hopefully catch a glimpse of the exceedingly well-camouflaged bears » Reindeer, Arctic foxes and seals are more common sightings

DAY 4 Morning pick-up in the 'Snow Weasel' (a tracked, all-terrain vehicle) for a trip to explore the ice cave inside the nearby glacier » Lunchtime transfer to airport for flight to Oslo and onto the UK

WHERE TO STAY

SVALBARD ARCTIC ADVENTURE

RADISSON SAS POLAR HOTEL
Originally home to Team USA during the 1994 Lillehammer Olympics, this hotel was subsequently reconstructed in Svalbard and offers a level of comfort you would not expect in the Arctic Circle.

CHARACTER Polar comfort **ROOMS** 95 **FEATURES** Central location; wireless broadband and satellite TV in all rooms; sauna; pub; good restaurant with panoramic views **LOCATION** Longyearbyen, the colourful little town that is the capital of Svalbard

SPITSBERGEN HOTEL
Overlooking Longyearbyen, the Spitsbergen Hotel was once the HQ and officers' mess for the local mining company. Now fully refurbished, it retains the character and feel of a gentlemen's club. *(Far page, middle)*

CHARACTER Old-school Arctic **ROOMS** 88 **FEATURES** Library with fireplace; bar; billiards room; gym; sauna; the best restaurant in town – with views to match **LOCATION** Longyearbyen

TAKE ME THERE
thebigshortbreak.co.uk
+44 (0)20 7978 7333

PS SVALBARD IS A TRUE WILDERNESS AND REQUIRES CARE AND RESPECT FROM VISITORS. STRICT RULES ON ENVIRONMENTAL PROTECTION MEAN IT'S EVEN ILLEGAL TO PICK A FLOWER.

EXPERIENCE THIS »

DRIVING AROUND HAVANA IN A VINTAGE 1950'S AMERICAN CAR (WITH A RUSSIAN ENGINE) IS A GREAT WAY TO SEE THE CITY. IF YOU HAPPEN TO BE THERE ON MAY DAY, CHECK OUT THE CELEBRATIONS ON THE PLAZA DE LA REVOLUCIÓN.

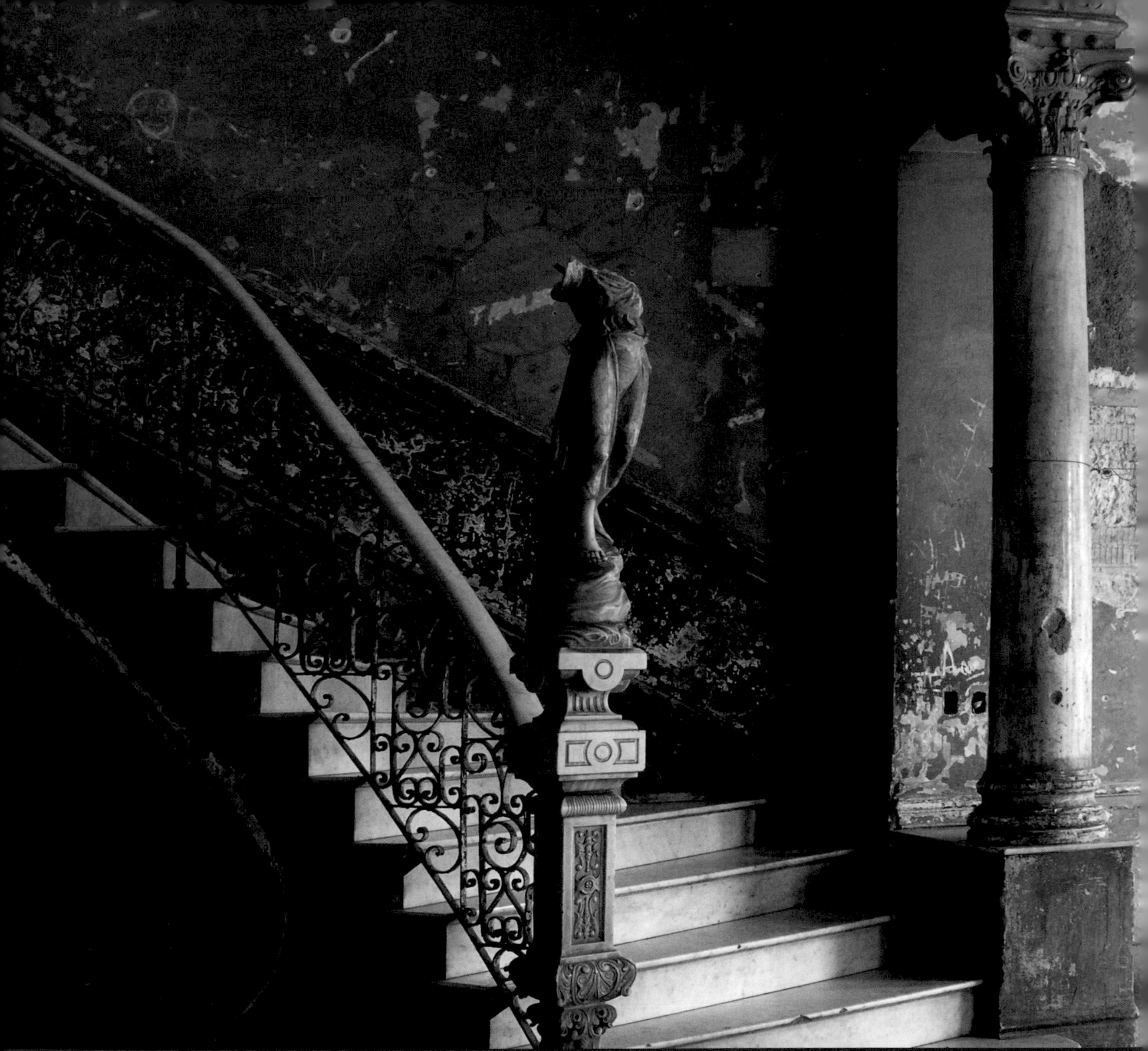

CUBA

Havana

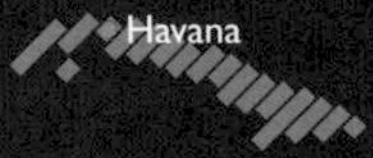

MUST SEE The faded
colonial grandeur of
Old Havana » The
Partagás cigar factory »
A six-piece *son* band
performing live **MUST DO**
Take an evening stroll
along the Malecón –
the seafront promenade
» Have a mojito on the

terrace of the Hotel
Nacional » Go deep-
sea fishing from the
Hemingway marina
(where else?)
RESTAURANTS/BARS
Eat at a *paladar* – small
restaurants run from
family homes (one
of the few private

businesses allowed to
operate). A good one
is La Guarida (Calle
Concordia 418, +537
863 7351) **SOUVENIRS**
Hand-rolled cigars
bought direct from the
factory » Havana Club
rum **BOOK TO PACK**
Our Man in Havana

by Graham Greene
DON'T FORGET... Your
passport when you go
deep-sea fishing – you
need it to prove you're
not a Cuban national
making a run for Florida
PRICE ■■■□□

BEST FOR… CHAMPAGNE SOCIALISTS » Divided by 90 miles of sea, and an ocean of mutual political distrust, Cuba and the United States remain stubbornly un-reconciled almost half a century since Castro's revolution. The long-predicted demise of the world's longest-serving leader may transform the Caribbean's largest island, but for the time being it continues defiantly – surviving, if not exactly thriving, as one of the last bastions of communism. Apart from the curiosity value of witnessing the effects of fifty years of a socialist economic model – and a US embargo – a few days in Havana makes an impressively big short break and offers *mucho* bang for your filthy American buck (or slightly more welcome pound). Currently being restored from an advanced state of decay, atmospheric Old Havana is a World Heritage Site, packed with colonial architecture from an era when the city was the 'Key to the New World'. Havana's status may have declined but it still ranks as one of the most interesting places in the western hemisphere, thanks not least to a vibrant cultural scene based on the islanders' Afro-Spanish heritage – anyone familiar with the Buena Vista Social Club will know that *Habañeros* know a thing or two about music. When you've seen the sights, relax on a beach just outside the city or, if you want a real challenge, try to find somewhere that doesn't claim a tenuous connection with Hemingway…

TAKE ME THERE
thebigshortbreak.co.uk
+44 (0)20 7978 7333

HAVANA: SALSA & CIGARS

✈ 9.5 HRS FROM UK

🧳 4 DAYS
2 DAYS OFF WORK

☀ MAR 19°/27°; APR 21°/29°
MAY 22°/30°

DAY 1 Morning flight from UK, arriving Havana mid-afternoon » Evening to sample live music or open-air cabaret » Overnight at Hotel Nacional or Saratoga

DAY 2 Guided walking tour of Old Havana including the cathedral, theatre, Plaza de Armas and the Museum of the Revolution » Siesta » Tour of a cigar factory and see sights such as El Morro fortress, the Bacardi building and the Capitol building (modelled, ironically, on Washington's)

DAY 3 Day to go fishing, with picnic lunch on board » Evening stroll along the Malecón » Experience more of Havana's nightlife

DAY 4 Morning on the beach » Lunch of fresh lobster salad » Transfer to airport for return flight home, arriving early next morning

HAVANA: SALSA & CIGARS

HOTEL SARATOGA
A modern reincarnation of the famous old Saratoga hotel, located opposite the Capitol building on the edge of the 'Old Havana' district, the historic heart of the city.

CHARACTER Contemporary colonial
ROOMS 96 **FEATURES** Prime central location; rooftop swimming pool and bar with great views over the city towards the Bay of Havana; gym; massage room; restaurant; two further bars; 24-hr room service; concierge
LOCATION Central Havana

HOTEL NACIONAL
A Havana institution, the Nacional occupies a landmark Art Deco building directly on the famous Malecón seafront in the Vedado district, the more modern part of the city. *(Far page, top right)*

CHARACTER Grande dame
ROOMS 457 **FEATURES** Seafront location; large gardens; two outdoor swimming pools; three restaurants; six bars; live music at the Cabaret Parisién; 24-hr room service; concierge
LOCATION Central Havana

TAKE ME THERE
thebigshortbreak.co.uk
+44 (0)20 7978 7333

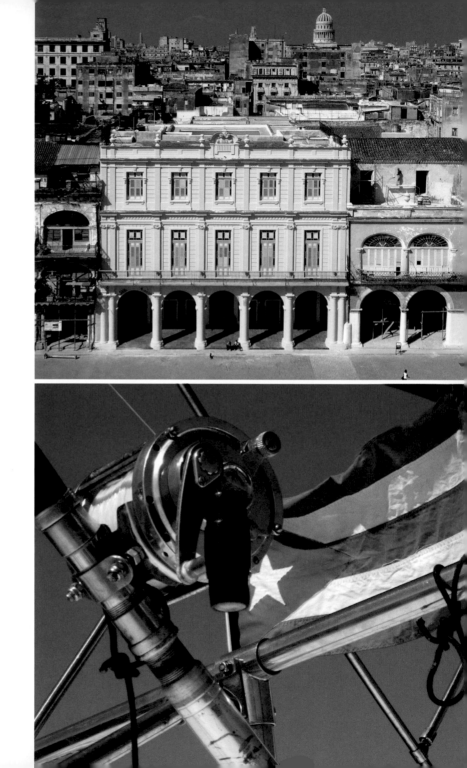

PS TOURISTS MUST PAY FOR EVERYTHING IN CUBAN CONVERTIBLE PESOS (CCP). STERLING CAN BE EXCHANGED COMMISSION-FREE, WHEREAS A COMMISSION OF 10% IS LEVIED ON US DOLLARS.

EXPERIENCE THIS »

DAWN OR DUSK ATOP A SAND DUNE OVERLOOKING
THE UBARI LAKES OR AKAKUS MOUNTAINS TAKES
SOME BEATING FOR AN 'OTHERWORLDLY' EXPERIENCE.
FIND A DUNE ALL TO YOURSELVES (NOT DIFFICULT)
AND LISTEN TO THE SILENCE.

LIBYA

Tripoli

Akakus Mountains

HIGHLIGHTS Leptis Magna— perhaps the best preserved Roman city in the world » The Ubari Lakes – picture-perfect desert oases » 8,000-year-old rock art, depicting scenes from a time when the Sahara was fertile **THINGS TO DO** Wander around the old amphitheatre at Sabratha » Admire the mosaics at Villa Silin » A 4WD safari in the Akakus Mountains **FOOD AND DRINK** Try fresh sardines, stuffed fennel bulbs and a glass of nut coffee at one of the restaurants in Tripoli's fish market **SOUVENIRS** A copy of the *Green Book* – the revolutionary theory of Colonel Gaddafi (could be a collector's item one day) » A piece of Tuareg silver jewellery or leatherwork **READING MATERIAL** *South from Barbary: Along the Slave Routes of the Libyan Sahara* by Justin Marozzi **ESSENTIALS** Your iPod or a good book for the long journeys through the desert **RATING** ■■■■□

BEST FOR… PIONEERS » Alcohol is strictly forbidden in Libya. If you can bear to read beyond this sentence, the cultural and visual rewards (not to mention the benefits to your liver) of a few days in North Africa's least discovered country will more than compensate for your abstinence. Libya's Mediterranean coast is home to arguably the most impressive classical ruins in the world. Either side of Tripoli are the ancient Roman cities of Sabratha and Leptis Magna (the latter being the birthplace of the 'African emperor', Septimius Severus, who died in York). Together, these were the 'Three Cities' from which modern Tripoli takes its name. Vandalised (predictably enough) by the Vandals, the cities were eventually abandoned and reclaimed by the desert sands. Their remarkably well-preserved ruins are all the more beautiful for being framed against a blue sea. Far to the south the Fezzan region, deep inside the Sahara, contains some of the most breathtaking desert scenery you could ever wish to see: classic palm-fringed oases, the dramatic rock formations of the Akakus Mountains and the endless golden sand sea of the Murzuq Dunes. Camp out under spectacular night skies and see prehistoric rock art which proves that drastic climate change is nothing new.

TAKE ME THERE
thebigshortbreak.co.uk
+44 (0)20 7978 7333

LIBYA: CLASSICAL CITIES & THE SAHARA

✈ 3.5 HRS FROM UK

🧳 5 DAYS
3 DAYS OFF WORK

☀ MAR 11°/19°, APR 14°/22°
MAY 16°/24°

DAY 1 Fly to Tripoli and transfer to Corinthia Bab Africa Hotel on the seafront » Lunch at the fish market » Afternoon to see the sights of Tripoli, including the triumphal arch of Marcus Aurelius, the *Assaraya al-Hamra* (Red Castle) and the Jamahiriya Museum.

DAY 2 Day trip to Leptis Magna: see the Baths of Hadrian and the Severan Arch » Return to Tripoli via Villa Silin » Evening flight to Sebha and overnight in the desert town of Germa

DAY 3 Drive on to Ghat, at the edge of the Akakus Mountains » Explore the desert with Tuareg guides by 4WD, horse or camel » Overnight under the stars at Dar Awiis

DAY 4 Drive back to Sebha, stopping at the Ubari Lakes near Germa » Picnic lunch by the Umm Al Maa' oasis » Fly back to Tripoli

DAY 5 Morning trip to Sabratha » Swim at Janzur beach on the way back » Transfer to airport for return flight to UK

ADD-ONS Optional extra days to travel via the Jebel Nafusa mountains to the historic Saharan town of Ghadames, or to fly to Benghazi and see the ancient Greek city of Cyrene

LIBYA: CLASSICAL CITIES & THE SAHARA

CORINTHIA BAB AFRICA
Libya's only genuine five-star hotel, the Corinthia Bab Africa is a striking modern building dominating the skyline of Tripoli's seafront.

CHARACTER Modern **ROOMS** 299 **FEATURES** Indoor and outdoor pools; gym; *hammam*; sauna; spa offering a variety of treatments; wide choice of restaurants; café; 24-hour room service; walking distance from the old town **LOCATION** Central Tripoli

DAR AWIIS DESERT CAMP
A remote desert camp surrounded by the dramatic scenery of the Akakus Mountains.

CHARACTER Tented desert camp **ROOMS** 34 **FEATURES** Simple but comfortable accommodation; sleep out under the stars; campfires; Italian food; Tuareg guides **LOCATION** Akakus Mountains

TAKE ME THERE
thebigshortbreak.co.uk
+44 (0)20 7978 7333

PS AS YOU CAN IMAGINE IN A COUNTRY SO UNACCUSTOMED TO TOURISM, CASH MACHINES ARE FEW AND FAR BETWEEN, SO MAKE SURE YOU HAVE PLENTY OF READIES TO HAND.

EXPERIENCE THIS »

DRIVE THROUGH THE MONT BLANC TUNNEL TO LA PALUD
AND TAKE A SERIES OF CABLE CARS, EACH SMALLER THAN THE
LAST, TO HELBRONNER POINT. FROM HERE, SKI THE TOULA
GLACIER AND ENJOY A FANTASTIC OFF-PISTE DESCENT
OF OVER 2,000 METRES, OFTEN IN DEEP POWDER.

AT A GLANCE

SPRING SKIING
IN CHAMONIX

FRANCE

Paris

Chamonix

MUST SEE The 360°
panorama from the
Aiguille du Midi » The
Mer de Glace – the
second largest glacier
in the Alps » The tips
of your skis bouncing
though fresh powder
MUST DO Discover an
off-piste paradise with

a professional guide –
the Vallée Blanche is
the best known, but
there are plenty to
choose from » Ditch
the skis and go para-
gliding or snowshoeing
» Get some fresh alpine
air in your lungs
RESTAURANTS/BARS

Enjoy magnificent
mountain scenery and
hearty Savoyard dishes
such as *tartiflette* from
the sun-terrace of Le
Panoramic restaurant
on the slopes of the
Brévent ski area (+33
(0)4 50 53 44 11)
SOUVENIRS A ski tan

and firmer thighs
BOOK TO PACK *Another
Long Day on the Piste*
by Will Randall DON'T
FORGET... A guide and
an avalanche transceiver,
shovel and probe for
off-piste adventures
PRICE ■ □ □ □ □

BEST FOR… SNOWMEN AND ICE MAIDENS » Since hosting the first Winter Olympics in 1924, Chamonix has been firmly established as one of the great ski resorts of the Alps. It is also one of the easiest to reach, being just an hour's drive from Geneva airport. The Chamonix Valley offers something for skiers of all levels, with over ninety miles of pistes ranging from gentle forest runs to steep blacks, but is chiefly renowned for its superb glacier and off-piste skiing. The most famous off-piste descent is the Vallée Blanche – a 12-mile, high-altitude route accessed via the spectacular cable-car ride to the Aiguille du Midi. Competent skiers can take the 'normal route' down, while experts can tackle the Envers du Plan descent. This and a host of other activities can be experienced with the help of Chamonix's highly experienced mountain guides. Heli-skiing in neighbouring Switzerland and Italy means you can go wherever the snow is best, and thanks to the big thermals generated by cold nights and warm days, Chamonix is also one of the world's top paragliding destinations. Further highlights range from peaceful, nocturnal snowshoeing by torch or moonlight to live music in the town's lively bars and clubs. All in all, Chamonix is the complete mountain resort.

TAKE ME THERE
thebigshortbreak.co.uk
+44 (0)20 7978 7333

SPRING SKIING IN CHAMONIX

✈ 1.5 HRS FROM UK

🧳 3 DAYS
0.5 DAY OFF WORK

☀ MAR -3°/10° ; APR -1°/14°
MAY 3°/18°

DAY 1 Afternoon flight to Geneva and transfer to Chamonix » Supper at one of the Hameau Albert 1er's excellent restaurants » Overnight at the Albert 1er

DAY 2 Full day of privately guided off-piste skiing, skinning or heli-skiing » Relaxing massage at the Albert 1er » Snow-shoe to a mountain restaurant for a supper of fondue or raclette, or enjoy après-ski in Chamonix

DAY 3 Day for more skiing or other activities: go paragliding or try speed-riding – the latest way to go down a mountain, involving a mixture of paragliding and skiing » Evening transfer back to Geneva for return flight home

SPRING SKIING
IN CHAMONIX

HAMEAU ALBERT IER
Chamonix's top hotel, the
Hameau Albert Ier offers a blend
of contemporary and traditional
luxury, with many rooms enjoying
views of Mont Blanc. The perfect
place to unwind after a long day
on the slopes. *(This page; far page,
top right and bottom left)*

CHARACTER Five-star chalet
ROOMS 36 **FEATURES** Indoor and
outdoor swimming pools; spa; sauna;
hammam; gym and climbing wall; two
excellent restaurants; 20,000-bottle
wine cellar **LOCATION** Chamonix

ADDITIONAL ACCOMMODATION
HOTEL MONT BLANC

TAKE ME THERE
thebigshortbreak.co.uk
+44 (0)20 7978 7333

PS BEAT THE MORNING
RUSH UP THE AIGUILLE DU
MIDI BY SPENDING THE NIGHT
IN THE COSMIQUES HUT ON
THE VALLÉE BLANCHE. ENJOY
THE DESCENT IN SPLENDID
ISOLATION THE NEXT MORNING.

EXPERIENCE THIS »

THE REEFS OFF THE COAST OF MOZAMBIQUE ARE SOME
OF THE MOST PRISTINE IN THE WORLD. SEEING A WHALE
SHARK (AT UP TO TWELVE METRES LONG, THE LARGEST
FISH IN THE SEA) IS ONE OF THE MOST MEMORABLE
ENCOUNTERS YOU CAN HAVE UNDERWATER – OR
ON LAND FOR THAT MATTER.

MUST SEE Shoals of
fish on the pristine
reefs of the Bazaruto
Archipelago » The
endangered dugong,
grazing on sea-grass »
Huge stands of flamingos
on Benguerra Island
MUST DO Go scuba-
diving on the ocean
side of Two-Mile Reef
and, with luck, see
a whale shark gliding
effortlessly past, almost
within touching distance
» Enjoy a castaway picnic
on a secluded beach »
Take a sundowner
cruise on a traditional
wooden sailing dhow »
Visit the villages
of the local Khokha
community on
Benguerra Island
RESTAURANTS/BARS
n/a SOUVENIRS A photo
of yourself having just
caught a 400lb black
marlin, shortly before
releasing it again

BOOK TO PACK A Fish
Caught in Time: The
Search for the Coelacanth
by Samantha Weinberg
DON'T FORGET... Your
diver's log book and
certification » Keen
fly-fishermen should
take their own tackle
PRICE ■ ■ ■ ■ ■

BEST FOR… LAID-BACK LUXURY » Benguerra is the second largest island of the Bazaruto Archipelago, which lies just off the southern coast of Mozambique and is one of the most idyllic spots along the entire coastline of East Africa. Bob Dylan, Mick Jagger & Co hung out here in the late sixties before civil war put Mozambique off-limits for the best part of two decades. With the country at peace again since the early nineties, those in the know are making their way back to a destination that offers a wonderful combination of marine safari and barefoot beach holiday. The archipelago lies within one of the most important marine conservation areas in the Indian Ocean, which translates into some of the best snorkelling and scuba diving in the world. The exceptionally healthy reefs are home to spectacular coral gardens and thousands of species of colourful fish with equally colourful names, such as 'Moorish idols' and 'barred sweetlips' (named in honour of Sir Mick, perhaps?). Dolphins, manta rays, whale sharks and five species of turtle are also abundant, while the shallows are one of the last refuges of the dugong (also known as a sea-cow, though more akin to an aquatic elephant). These waters also offer outstanding deep-sea fishing (on a strict 'catch & release' basis), or you can just get horizontal on the deserted white sand beaches.

TAKE ME THERE
thebigshortbreak.co.uk
+44 (0)20 7978 7333

INDIAN OCEAN SAFARI

✈ 11 HRS FROM UK
1.5 HRS TRANSFER

🧳 4 DAYS
2 DAYS OFF WORK

☀ MAR 22°/31°: APR 20°/29°
MAY 18°/27°

DAY 1 Arrive in Johannesburg after overnight flight » Connect to Vilanculos and transfer by boat or seaplane to Benguerra Island » Lunch of fresh seafood » Swim and laze on the beach » Overnight at Benguerra Lodge

DAY 2 Enjoy a day of world-class diving, snorkelling and fishing » Relaxing massage » Take an evening dhow cruise to see the flamingos » Supper of barbecued crayfish and coconut rice on the beach

DAY 3 Morning 4WD tour or nature walk on the island, with visit to local village » Picnic lunch on a private beach (radio when you're ready to be collected) » Rest of day to relax

DAY 4 Morning to go sea kayaking, sailing, snorkelling or saltwater fly-fishing » Freshly grilled fish and chilled rosé for lunch » Mid-afternoon transfer back to Johannesburg for return flight home, arriving early next morning

WHERE TO STAY

INDIAN OCEAN
SAFARI

BENGUERRA LODGE

An immaculate, boutique beach
retreat set on a beautiful bay on
the island of Benguerra, part of
the Bazaruto Archipelago.

CHARACTER Beach lodge **ROOMS** 14
FEATURES Private white sand beach;
fully equipped dive centre; freshwater
swimming pool; small spa; snorkelling;
sea kayaking; sailing; saltwater fly-fishing
and deep-sea fishing; nature walks;
picnics on neighbouring islands; bar;
sunset dhow cruises **LOCATION**
Benguerra Island *(Previous page; this
page, bottom)*

ADDITIONAL ACCOMMODATION
MARLIN LODGE (BENGUERRA ISLAND)

TAKE ME THERE
thebigshortbreak.co.uk
+44 (0)20 7978 7333

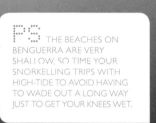

PS THE BEACHES ON BENGUERRA ARE VERY SHALLOW, SO TIME YOUR SNORKELLING TRIPS WITH HIGH-TIDE TO AVOID HAVING TO WADE OUT A LONG WAY JUST TO GET YOUR KNEES WET.

EXPERIENCE THIS »

TREK ON THE RUGGED FLANKS OF THE TOUBKAL MASSIF AND STAY OVERNIGHT IN REMOTE VILLAGES – A PERFECT COMBINATION WITH THE SIGHTS AND SOUNDS OF NEARBY MARRAKECH.

TREK THE
HIGH ATLAS

MOROCCO

Marrakech
Mt Toubkal

MUST SEE The view
from the summit of
Jebel Toubkal – on a
clear day you can see
the Sahara » Goatherds
shepherding their flocks
along the mountain
slopes » Stunning
mountain scenery from
the Tizi n'Tamatert

pass **MUST DO** An
overnight trek, staying
at the Toubkal Lodge
in the spectacular
Azzadene valley » Drink
from the spring at Sidi
Chamarouch – reputed
to have restorative
powers for weary legs
» Sip mint tea on the

roof terrace of Kasbah
du Toubkal and admire
the view **RESTAURANTS/
BARS** Supper on the
terrace at Kasbah
Tamadot **SOUVENIRS** A
djellaba – the traditional,
hooded woollen robe
worn by the Berbers.
Or the obligatory carpet

BOOK TO PACK *Lords
of the Atlas: The Rise
and Fall of the House
of Glaoua* 1893-1956 by
Gavin Maxwell **DON'T
FORGET…** Head-torch –
indispensable for
camping in the
mountains
PRICE ■■□□□

BEST FOR… GETTING AWAY FROM IT ALL » Most people visit Morocco to spend time in its medieval cities such as Fès, Meknès and Marrakech, but to experience a completely different and altogether more tranquil aspect of the country, the High Atlas Mountains are the place to head for. Easily accessed from Marrakech, these snow-capped peaks, known to the Berbers as 'Idraren Draren' (Mountains of Mountains) are the perfect antidote to the hustle and bustle of the cities. Perched among the foothills, restored kasbahs provide atmospheric lodgings and make ideal bases from which to enjoy some of the best trekking in the world. Walk with local guides along winding mule trails, through orchards, terraced fields and tiny Berber villages, stopping for picnic lunches by streams or waterfalls. The spring months are especially beautiful, when the blossom is thick on the apple and cherry trees and the alpine flowers are in bloom. The walking ranges from gentle rambles to extended overnight treks, including an ascent of Jebel Toubkal – at 4,167m North Africa's highest peak. Alternatively, the mountains are the perfect place to chill out for a couple of days, enjoying peaceful surroundings, clean air and inspiring views.

TAKE ME THERE
thebigshortbreak.co.uk
+44 (0)20 7978 7333

TREK THE HIGH ATLAS

✈ 3.5 HRS FROM UK

🧳 5 DAYS
3 DAYS OFF WORK

☀ MAR 2°/21°: APR 3°/23°
MAY 7°/26°

DAY 1 Fly to Marrakech » Transfer to a riad in the old *medina* » Spend the evening immersed in the sights, sounds and smells of the Djemaa el Fna Square » Overnight in Marrakech

DAY 2 Breakfast on roof terrace of your riad » Scenic drive to the High Atlas Mountains, stopping at the livestock market in Asni » Continue to Kasbah Toubkal or Kasbah Tamadot » Settle in, relax or go for an evening stroll

DAY 3 Full day's guided walking in the mountains, with a picnic lunch » Return to the kasbah for a well-earned steam in the *hammam* and a supper of traditional Berber food

DAY 4 Day of trekking, or relax at the kasbah and wander round Imlil village » If staying at Kasbah Tamadot, early morning hot-air balloon flights are possible, with breakfast in a Berber village afterwards

DAY 5 Breakfast on the terrace, enjoying the mountain views one last time before transfer back to Marrakech for return flight home

ADD-ONS Optional extra days for overnight treks, trips to the desert, or time in Marrakech

TREK THE HIGH ATLAS

KASBAH DU TOUBKAL
A historic former fortress perched on a rocky outcrop at the foot of Jebel Toubkal. The kasbah overlooks the Berber village of Imlil and has panoramic views of the surrounding mountains. *(Previous page; this page, top)*

CHARACTER Mountain lodge
ROOMS 17 **FEATURES** Guided walks; mule and camel trekking expeditions in the mountains (including ascent of Jebel Toubkal); horse riding; *hammam*; authentic Berber food; roof-terrace with superb views; relaxed, down-to-earth atmosphere; peace and seclusion
LOCATION Toubkal National Park, High Atlas Mountains

KASBAH TAMADOT
An attractively converted kasbah with five-star facilities set in stunning surroundings in the foothills of the High Atlas Mountains. Part of Sir Richard Branson's property collection. *(This page, bottom; far page, bottom left and top left)*

CHARACTER Mountain retreat
ROOMS 18 **FEATURES** Beautiful building amid beautiful scenery; large terraced gardens; indoor and outdoor pools; sundecks; two floodlit tennis courts; spa; sauna; *hammam*; gym; excellent restaurant; roof-terrace with great views; hot-air ballooning (of course); horse riding; variety of local excursions
LOCATION Near Asni, Atlas Mountains

ADDITIONAL ACCOMMODATION
KASBAH SAMRA (ATLAS MOUNTAINS)
VILLA DES ORANGERS (MARRAKECH)
JNANE TAMSNA (MARRAKECH)

TAKE ME THERE
thebigshortbreak.co.uk
+44 (0)20 7978 7333

P.S ALWAYS TAKE UP THE OPTION OF A MULE WHEN GOING ON A LENGTHY TREK – IT NOT ONLY CARRIES YOUR PACK BUT PROVIDES WELCOME TRANSPORT IF AND WHEN YOUR LEGS NEED A REST.

EXPERIENCE THIS »
WATCH A HAWK DISPLAY ITS AERIAL AGILITY AS IT
SWOOPS ON TO A PIECE OF MEAT BEING WHIRLED
AROUND ON THE END OF A STRING BY ITS HANDLER.

BEST FOR... ARABIAN NIGHTS » Underwater hotels, artificial islands, mile-high skyscrapers and indoor ski resorts are the things that have put modern Dubai on the map, but less than an hour's drive from the futuristic architecture and sprawling shopping malls lies a taste of what this small emirate was all about before the discovery of oil. The stillness of the desert makes a welcome contrast to the frenetic activity of the coast, and the views stretch for miles across open plains and dune belts to the distant Hajar Mountains. From a couple of luxurious desert retreats the pristine landscapes of the Dubai Desert Conservation Reserve can be explored on horseback, camelback or on guided nature walks. Discover the indigenous desert flora and fauna, including the endangered Arabian oryx, sand gazelle, and birds such as bee-eaters, hoopoe and desert wheatear, and go on excursions to the mountains and wadis. Other activities range from traditional pursuits such as falconry and archery to more modern diversions including sand skiing, quad biking and 4WD dune safaris. Alternatively, you can just relax by the pool, be pampered at the spa, and enjoy the all but guaranteed sunshine. Before flying home, spend a day or two at one of the beach resorts of the Gulf coast.

TAKE ME THERE
thebigshortbreak.co.uk
+44 (0)20 7978 7333

DUBAI DESERT ESCAPE

✈ 7 HRS FROM UK

💼 4 DAYS
2 DAYS OFF WORK

☀ MAR 16°/27°; APR 18°/30°
MAY 22°/34°

DAY 1 Arrive into Dubai after overnight flight » Transfer to the desert » Rest of day to relax by the pool or enjoy spa treatments » Overnight at Al Maha or Bab Al Shams

DAY 2 Morning horse ride or camel trek in the desert » Relax by the pool or enjoy spa treatments » Evening falconry display or guided nature walk with sundowner drinks on the dunes

DAY 3 4WD excursion to the historic fortified village of Hatta in the mountains » Lunch in a palm-fringed wadi » Return via the picturesque Al Ain region and see the views from Jebel Hafeet

DAY 4 Morning to try archery or relax and enjoy the panoramic views of the desert » Transfer back to Dubai airport for return flight home

ADD-ONS Optional extra days on the beach or to enjoy the sights and shopping of Dubai

DUBAI DESERT ESCAPE

AL MAHA DESERT RESORT & SPA

Designed to resemble a Bedouin encampment (though no Bedouin ever lived quite like this) Al Maha is a multi award-winning resort set in peaceful isolation on a 225 sq km desert reserve. *(This page, bottom; far page, middle)*

CHARACTER Luxury tented desert camp **ROOMS** 40 **FEATURES** All rooms with private swimming pools; staff-to-room ratio of 4:1; excellent restaurant (and private dining on the outdoor decks of the rooms); spa offering a variety of massage and beauty treatments; sauna; steam room; Jacuzzi; ice-cold plunge pool; library; gym; falconry; camel treks; horse riding; archery; nature walks; 4WD desert safaris and a variety of off-site excursions. (All facilities exclusively for use of resident guests. No children under 12.) **LOCATION** Dubai Desert Conservation Reserve

BAB AL SHAMS DESERT RESORT & SPA

An atmospheric, five-star desert resort with first-class facilities, styled as a traditional Arabian fortress. *(This page, top)*

CHARACTER Resort **ROOMS** 115 **FEATURES** Stunning infinity pool with swim-up pool-bar; spa offering a variety of massage and beauty treatments; refreshing 'rain room'; gym; shaded children's pool and Sinbad Kids' Club; guided horse riding with genuine Arabian horses; camel rides; archery; falconry displays; 4WD desert excursions; several restaurants; rooftop cocktail bar; 24-hr room service **LOCATION** In the desert, 45 minutes from Dubai

ADDITIONAL ACCOMMODATION

ROYAL MIRAGE (ON THE COAST)
RITZ CARLTON (ON THE COAST)

TAKE ME THERE

thebigshortbreak.co.uk
+44 (0)20 7978 7333

PS HOLD ON TIGHT
WHEN YOU MOUNT A CAMEL,
AS YOU WILL BE PITCHED
FORWARDS THEN BACKWARDS
WHEN IT STANDS UP. AFTER
THAT IT'S (SLIGHTLY) MORE
COMFORTABLE.

CAR-FREE VENICE IS PERFECT FOR WALKING, AND A
SUNSET STROLL ALONG THE ZATTERE QUAY TO THE
PUNTA DELLA DOGANA IS A MUST. DRINK IN THE VIEWS
(AND THE BELLINIS) AT ONE OF THE CANAL-SIDE CAFÉS.

VENICE: BRIDGES &
BELLINIS

ITALY

Venice

Rome

MUST SEE The Sala
dello Scudo (colloquially
known as the 'map
room') in the Doge's
Palace » The Arsenale –
where Venice's merchant
and military fleets
were once built » The
city floodlit at night
MUST DO Climb the bell

tower of San Giorgio
Maggiore for fantastic
views » Visit the fish
market at Rialto –
Venice's historic
commercial centre »
Take a boat trip to the
islands of the lagoon
RESTAURANTS/BARS
L'Osteria di Santa

Marina is popular with
Venetians and serves
excellent fish (Campo
Santa Marina 5911,
Castello +39 (0)41
528 5239) **SOUVENIRS**
Hand-blown glass from
the island of Murano,
in Venice's lagoon »
Hand-made marbled

paper **BOOK TO PACK**
The Merchant of Venice
by William Shakespeare
DON'T FORGET Your
other half » Wellies in
case of the spring tides
known as *acqua alta*
(high water)
PRICE ■ ■ □ □ □

BEST FOR… LOVERS » The amazing thing about Venice (apart from the obvious fact that the streets are full of water) is that it exists at all. How did a settlement founded by a group of refugees on a few swampy islands become *La Serenissima Repubblica* – the centre of a maritime empire that once dominated the Mediterranean? Venice is, quite simply, special – one of those places that have to be seen at least once in your life – and spring is one of the best times to visit, before the heat and crowds of summer make sightseeing a struggle. Those sights are too numerous to mention, but a few that should not be missed are the Doge's Palace, the Byzantine masterpiece of St Mark's Basilica with its gilded mosaic interiors, the Scuola Grande di San Rocco with its paintings by Tintoretto, and the Rialto Bridge – arguably the most beautiful of the 400-odd bridges that bind the city together across some 150 canals. Spare some time for just losing yourself in the urban labyrinth – hardly any corner of Venice lacks beauty or charm – and then catch the *vaporetto* (water-bus) to other islands in the lagoon for some open space and panoramas of the greatest sight of all: a city of such intense beauty, seemingly floating on the water.

TAKE ME THERE
thebigshortbreak.co.uk
+44 (0)20 7978 7333

VENICE: BRIDGES & BELLINIS

✈ 2.5 HRS FROM UK

🧳 3 DAYS
1 DAY OFF WORK

☀ MAR 5°/12°; APR 10°/17°
MAY 14°/21°

DAY 1 Fly to Venice's Marco Polo airport » Transfer by *motoscafo* (water-taxi) to Hotel Cipriani or Ca Maria Adele » Afternoon to explore the city and go for a gondola ride » Supper overlooking the water

DAY 2 Visit the islands of Murano and Burano in the lagoon by *vaporetto* or private Riva motor launch » Lunch at the Lido beach » Afternoon visit to the San Trovaso gondola workshop

DAY 3 See Old Masters at the Accademia or modern art at the Guggenheim » Explore the islands of Giudecca or San Pietro, and visit the market on Via Garibaldi » Transfer to airport for return flight home

VENICE: BRIDGES & BELLINIS

HOTEL CIPRIANI

One of the great hotels of the world, the legendary Cipriani is a Venice institution. The hotel occupies a cluster of historic buildings surrounded by gardens at the tip of Giudecca Island.

CHARACTER Unique **ROOMS** 104
FEATURES Stunning, peaceful location away from the crowds of the main island; fantastic views across the water to St Mark's Square; gardens and vineyard; Olympic size saltwater swimming pool; the only tennis court in central Venice; beauty treatments and massages; hair salon; gym; formal and informal restaurants with lagoon-side dining; two bars; 24-hour free boat service to St Mark's Square; boat trips to other islands; concierge **LOCATION** Giudecca Island

CA MARIA ADELE

A beautifully designed boutique hotel in a restored 16th-century *palazzo*, tucked away in the charming Dorsoduro district of Venice.

CHARACTER Boutique *palazzo*
ROOMS 14 **FEATURES** Historic building; waterside entrance for arrival by boat; views of the canals and the neighbouring church of Santa Maria della Salute; breakfast room and bar with terrace; two minutes by boat to St Mark's Square **LOCATION** Dorsoduro district

TAKE ME THERE

thebigshortbreak.co.uk
+44 (0)20 7978 7333

PS DO AS THE LOCALS DO: STAY TO THE RIGHT WHEN WALKING ACROSS BRIDGES, AND DON'T SIT DOWN ON THE *TRAGHETTO* (THE GONDOLA-FERRY ACROSS THE GRAND CANAL).

EXPERIENCE THIS »

GIANT MORAY EELS, HAMMERHEAD AND LEOPARD
SHARKS, BARRACUDA AND SPECTACULAR SOFT CORALS
ARE JUST A FEW OF THE UNDERWATER HIGHLIGHTS OF
RAS MOHAMMED – CONSISTENTLY RANKED AMONGST
THE TOP DIVE SITES IN THE WORLD.

AT A GLANCE

PYRAMIDS &
THE RED SEA

EGYPT

Cairo
Sharm el Sheikh

MUST SEE The Great Pyramid of Khufu – sole survivor of the Seven Wonders of the Ancient World » The Royal Mummy Room and treasures of Tutankhamun in the Egyptian Museum » The colourful reefs of the Ras Mohammed National Park MUST DO Drift down the Nile in a private *felucca* (traditional wooden sailing boat) » Dive the amazingly colourful 'Small Crack' – often described as a flooded florist's » Drink mint tea over a game of backgammon at a Cairo café RESTAURANTS/BARS n/a SOUVENIRS Not a miniature sphinx. Instead, try something from the Khan el-Khalili souq – Cairo's most famous market BOOK TO PACK *The Cairo Trilogy* by Naguib Mahfouz (adults) » *Think Like an Egyptian, 100 Hieroglyphs* by Barry Kemp (adults/kids) DON'T FORGET… Your underwater camera PRICE ■■■■□

BEST FOR… DIVERS AND EGYPTOLOGISTS » For families with children who are old enough to scuba dive and to appreciate (or at least not resent) a bit of culture, Egypt makes the ideal destination. Its Red Sea coast offers undoubtedly the best diving within easy reach of Europe. Sharm el Sheikh, at the tip of the Sinai Peninsula, and Hurghada, just across the Gulf of Suez, both have excellent, family-friendly resorts with fully equipped dive centres for scuba instruction and exploring the beautiful underwater world. Unlike many other places, the coral reefs here are still in good health and harbour almost as many fish species as Australia's Great Barrier Reef, while the numerous wrecks that lie in these warm, shallow waters add extra interest to the diving. For kids too young to dive, there is still great snorkelling and all kinds of other activities on land and sea. Travel via Cairo and take in the pyramids and the Sphinx at Giza. Stand and admire the Great Pyramid of Khufu, a structure which consists of over two million blocks of stone and has stood for more than forty-five centuries – for most of which time it was the world's tallest building. As the Arab proverb goes: 'Man fears time, but time fears the pyramids.'

TAKE ME THERE
thebigshortbreak.co.uk
+44 (0)20 7978 7333

PYRAMIDS &
THE RED SEA

✈ 5 HRS FROM UK

🧳 6 DAYS
3 DAYS OFF WORK

☀ MAR 11°/24°; APR 14°/28°
MAY 17°/33°

DAY 1 Evening flight to Cairo » Transfer to the Mena House Oberoi, right next to the pyramids at Giza

DAY 2 Wake to stunning views of the pyramids » Private guided visit to the Egyptian Museum » Lunch on board a private *felucca* on the Nile » Afternoon visit to pyramids and Sphinx » Fly to Sharm el Sheikh or Hurghada

DAY 3 Full day's privately guided diving in Ras Mohammed National Park or around the island of Tiran – two of the most famous dive sites in the Red Sea » For non-divers, the snorkelling is spectacular too

DAY 4 Another day's diving or snorkelling » Turtles, eagle rays, giant moray eels and the superbly camouflaged crocodilefish are among the many species to look for » Advanced divers can try a night dive

DAY 5 Day off diving to allow for restrictions on flying following diving » Relax on the beach or at the spa, enjoy watersports, play golf or ride camels

DAY 6 Morning transfer back to Sharm el Sheikh or Hurghada for direct flight home

PYRAMIDS & THE RED SEA

FOUR SEASONS SHARM EL SHEIKH
A first class, family-friendly resort with superb all-round facilities, including its own scuba diving centre. *(Far page, middle left)*

CHARACTER Beach resort **ROOMS** 136
FEATURES Excellent family and children's facilities (including family suites or connecting rooms and babysitting service); private sandy beach; swimming pool; dive centre; watersports; spa; gym; choice of restaurants; floodlit tennis courts; boat trips and jeep excursions around Sinai; concierge **LOCATION** Sharm el Sheikh

OBEROI SAHL HASHEESH
A luxurious, all-suite resort with an in-house dive centre, set in 48 acres of palm-filled grounds on Egypt's Red Sea coast. *(Far page, bottom right)*

CHARACTER Beach resort **ROOMS** 102
FEATURES Private sandy beach; swimming pool; dive centre; spa; gym; tennis court; kids' club with bowling, slides and mini-basketball; three restaurants; bar; desert safaris and full-day excursions to Coptic monasteries or Luxor; concierge **LOCATION** Six miles south of Hurghada

MENA HOUSE OBEROI
A luxurious resort based around a historic 19th-century building, set amid 40 acres of landscaped gardens in the shadow of the Great Pyramids.

CHARACTER Resort hotel **ROOMS** 523
FEATURES Swimming pool; 18-hole golf course; tennis courts; gym; jogging track; horse and camel riding; several restaurants serving Egyptian, Indian and European cuisine; two bars; nightclub **LOCATION** Giza

ADDITIONAL ACCOMMODATION
FOUR SEASONS NILE PLAZA (CAIRO)

TAKE ME THERE
thebigshortbreak.co.uk
+44 (0)20 7978 7333

PS THE DIVING IN THE DEAD SEA GETS BETTER AND BETTER AS SPRING PROGRESSES, SO FOR OPTIMUM VISIBILITY IT'S WORTH CONSIDERING GOING IN MAY, EVEN THOUGH IT'S PRETTY HOT BY THEN.

ANDALUCIAN ESCAPE

EXPERIENCE THIS »

SPRING IS THE TIME TO GET OUT INTO THE COUNTRY IN ANDALUCIA – GO WALKING IN THE SIERRAS (WHERE THE WILDFLOWERS ARE FANTASTIC) RIDE A HORSE ALONG THE ENDLESS SAND DUNE BEACHES OF THE COSTA DE LA LUZ, OR WATCH THE HONEY BUZZARDS, EAGLES AND VULTURES MIGRATING NORTHWARDS ACROSS THE STRAITS OF GIBRALTAR.

MUST SEE The Mezquita, Córdoba's huge mosque (now a cathedral) » A performance of the 'dancing horses' at the Royal Andalucian School of Equestrian Art in Jerez » The Alhambra and the Generalife gardens in Granada »

The panoramic views from the Puente Nuevo bridge across the ravine in Ronda **MUST DO** Visit one of the picturesque *pueblos blancos* ('white villages') » Climb to the top of *La Giralda*, the 12th century Moorish minaret in Seville » Visit the

sherry *bodegas* in Jerez **RESTAURANTS/BARS** La Trastienda – one of the best seafood tapas bars in Seville (Calle Alfalfa 1) **SOUVENIRS** Lace shawls » Hand-painted Andalucian pottery » Woollen rugs from Grazalema

BOOK TO PACK *South from Granada* by Gerald Brenan **DON'T FORGET...** To book early for the *Feria de Abril* (April Fair) in Seville – the week-long party that draws people from all over Spain and beyond **PRICE** ■ □ □ □ □

BEST FOR… A SPRING BREAK (NOT THE AMERICAN SORT) »

The kind of place northern Europeans dream of on cold, rainy days, Andalucia is prime Big Short Break country. One of the continent's most varied regions, it pretty much has it all: a wealth of history and culture, idyllic countryside dotted with the characteristic *pueblos blancos*, and activities ranging from kite-surfing on the beaches of the Costa de la Luz to skiing in the Sierra Nevada. Seville, Córdoba and Granada are home to superb examples of Islamic architecture – the legacy of over seven centuries of Moorish rule – as well as Roman remains (three Roman emperors were Spanish-born) and monuments from the days when Andalucia was the gateway to the New World. Spring is the ideal time to go, when the almond and orange trees are in blossom and the temperature is not too oppressive for sightseeing. Rural Andalucia offers great walking and horse riding trails in the hills, and natural refuges such as the renowned wetlands of the Coto Doñana National Park, one of the most important wildlife sanctuaries in Europe. If pure relaxation is what you're looking for, lazing in the garden of a restored hacienda, eating tapas and sipping chilled sherry from the vineyards of nearby Jerez is hard to beat.

TAKE ME THERE
thebigshortbreak.co.uk
+44 (0)20 7978 7333

ANDALUCIAN ESCAPE

✈ 2.5 HRS FROM UK

🧳 4 DAYS
1 DAY OFF WORK

☀ MAR 9°/20°; APR 11°/24°; MAY 13°/77°

DAY 1 Evening flight to Seville and transfer to the Hacienda San Rafael or Hacienda Benazuza » Drinks and supper at the hotel (if staying at Hacienda Benazuza, try the Michelin-starred La Alqueria restaurant – sibling of the famed El Bulli restaurant near Barcelona, often voted best restaurant in the world)

DAY 2 Day at leisure to explore the Andalucian countryside on foot or horseback, visit the cities or the coast, or just relax by the pool » In the evening, head into Seville for tapas, followed by a flamenco show in the Triana district or a boat trip on the Guadalquivir river

DAY 3 Day trip to Jerez de la Frontera, Córdoba or Granada (by train) – or even across the Straits of Gibraltar to Tangiers » Alternatively, relax amid the olive groves of the hacienda and soak up the spring sunshine

DAY 4 Go kite-surfing at Tarifa or walking in the beautiful Sierra de Grazalema Natural Park » Lunch by the sea, or in one of the *pueblos blancos* » Afternoon transfer back to Seville for return flight home

ADD-ONS Optional extra day with overnight stay in Granada

ANDALUCIAN ESCAPE

HACIENDA DE SAN RAFAEL

A family-run, former olive farm in a beautiful rural setting, perfectly placed for exploring the various attractions of western Andalucia. *(Far page, top right)*

CHARACTER Country house **ROOMS** 14 **FEATURES** Relaxed, rustic atmosphere; five acres of gardens; three swimming pools; *padel* tennis court; yoga; massages; library; restaurant; bar; horse riding; bespoke excursions with private guides **LOCATION** Between Seville and Jerez

HACIENDA BENAZUZA

A historic Moorish hacienda dating back to the 10th century, now transformed into one of Andalucia's most luxurious hideaways. *(This page, top)*

CHARACTER Five-star hacienda **ROOMS** 44 **FEATURES** Large gardens with palm trees, orange groves and fountains; swimming pool with pool bar; three restaurants (including La Alqueria, with two Michelin stars); mini-spa with sauna, Jacuzzi, Turkish bath and massage service; tennis court; billiards room; two bars; concierge **LOCATION** Sanlúcar La Mayor, just outside Seville

ADDITIONAL ACCOMMODATION

TRASIERRA (IN THE SIERRA MORENA)
PALACIO DE LOS PATOS (GRANADA)

TAKE ME THERE

thebigshortbreak.co.uk
+44 (0)20 7978 7333

PS WHEN ENJOYING A TRADITIONAL *TAPEO* (TAPAS BAR CRAWL) AS A GENERAL RULE OF THUMB, THE NOISIER THE BAR, AND THE MORE SAWDUST THERE IS ON THE FLOOR, THE BETTER THE TAPAS.

SKELETON COAST SAFARI

EXPERIENCE THIS »

DRIVING AROUND THE DESERT WITH STRANGE AND
BEAUTIFUL NEW LANDSCAPES OPENING UP BEFORE YOU,
IT CAN FEEL LIKE YOU ARE THE FIRST PERSON TO EXPLORE
THIS PRISTINE ENVIRONMENT – AND NOT THAT MANY
PEOPLE HAVE (EXCEPT FOR THESE ONES OF COURSE).

SKELETON COAST SAFARI

SKELETON COAST SAFARI CAMPS
A series of remote camps, scenically located at intervals along the Skeleton Coast. The camps are operated by the Schoeman family – pioneers in the exploration of the Skeleton Coast since the 1970s, who have an unrivalled knowledge of this unique wilderness.

CHARACTER Tented desert camps
ROOMS 4 **FEATURES** Unique access to a variety of different locations along the Skeleton Coast; expert guiding on land and by air with the Schoeman family; simple but comfortable accommodation
LOCATION Skeleton Coast

WILDERNESS SKELETON COAST CAMP
A luxury tented camp built on an island in the dry Kumib river-bed and surrounded by beautiful desert scenery.

CHARACTER Tented safari camp
ROOMS 6 **FEATURES** Comfortable, spacious tents on raised wooden platforms; en-suite bathrooms with showers; indoor and outdoor dining areas; bar; 4WD desert excursions
LOCATION Skeleton Coast National Park

ADDITIONAL ACCOMMODATION
SERRA CAFEMA (This page, top)

TAKE ME THERE
thebigshortbreak.co.uk
+44 (0)20 7978 7333

PS TEMPERATURES VARY ENORMOUSLY IN THE DESERT. ANYTHING FROM A FEW DEGREES ABOVE FREEZING TO THE HIGH 30's IS POSSIBLE. TAKE SOME WARM CLOTHES AND LOTS OF LAYERS TO COPE.

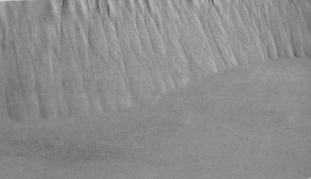

EXPERIENCE THIS

A DAWN HOT-AIR BALLOON FLIGHT, FLYING LOW OVER THE STRANGE, LUNAR LANDSCAPES AND LANDING FOR BREAKFAST AMONGST THE WEIRD ROCK FORMATIONS, IS THE BEST WAY TO TAKE IN THIS UNIQUE DESTINATION.

CAPPADOCIA ADVENTURE

YUNAK EVLERI
A truly unique hotel, consisting of six cave-houses and a 19th-century Greek mansion set at the foot of towering cliffs.

CHARACTER Cave-dweller chic **ROOMS** 27 **FEATURES** Some rooms are cave-rooms burrowed deep into the cliffs and date back to the 5th and 6th centuries; modern bathrooms; private balconies or patios; panoramic rooftop restaurant **LOCATION** In the village of Ürgüp

SACRED HOUSE
An intimate boutique hotel housed in an attractive, 250-year-old Greek mansion, beautifully furnished with antique pieces. *(Far page, middle)*

CHARACTER Boutique **ROOMS** 7 **FEATURES** Historic building; shaded courtyard; terrace; good restaurant; Jacuzzis in bathrooms **LOCATION** In the village of Ürgüp

ADDITIONAL ACCOMMODATION
MUSEUM HOTEL (CAPPADOCIA)
ANATOLIAN HOUSES (CAPPADOCIA)
FOUR SEASONS (ISTANBUL)
A'JIA HOTEL (ISTANBUL)

TAKE ME THERE
thebigshortbreak.co.uk
+44 (0)20 7978 7333

PS VISIT THE VALLEYS EARLY IN THE MORNING TO AVOID THE MIDDAY SUN AND THEN EXPLORE THE UNDERGROUND CITIES AT THE END OF THE DAY TO AVOID THE DAY-TRIPPERS.

EXPERIENCE THIS »

EXPLORE THE VASTNESS OF THE DESERT LANDSCAPE
IN JORDAN'S WADI RUM, ONE OF THE LOCATIONS FROM
WHICH LAWRENCE OF ARABIA LED THE ARAB REVOLT
DURING WORLD WAR ONE.

PETRA & WADI RUM

FOUR SEASONS AMMAN

Amman's finest hotel, with five-star facilities and panoramic views.

CHARACTER Contemporary **ROOMS** 192 **FEATURES** Indoor and outdoor swimming pools; spa; gym; four restaurants; concierge **LOCATION** Central Amman

BEDOUIN CAMP

A completely private Bedouin camp, offering simple but comfortable accommodation in the silent expanses of the open desert. *(Far page, top left)*

CHARACTER Tented camp **ROOMS** Just yours **FEATURES** Peace and quiet; awesome night skies; campfire; traditional food; basic bathroom facilities **LOCATION** Wadi Rum

MÖVENPICK RESORT, PETRA

The leading hotel in the Petra area, located right next to the entrance to the ancient city.

CHARACTER Contemporary **ROOMS** 183 **FEATURES** Swimming pool; steam bath; several restaurants; bar; tea-room and roof garden **LOCATION** Petra

KEMPINSKI HOTEL ISHTAR, DEAD SEA

A stylish new resort, set on the shores of the Dead Sea. Accommodation is divided between the main Arabesque hotel and the more luxurious Ishtar Villas. *(Far page, bottom left)*

CHARACTER Luxury spa resort **ROOMS** 318 **FEATURES** Comprehensive spa offering treatments based on the Dead Sea's mineral-laden water and mud; private beach; *hammam* and ice-cave; nine pools; tennis; kids' club; cinema **LOCATION** Dead Sea

TAKE ME THERE

thebigshortbreak.co.uk
+44 (0)20 7978 7333

PS WHEN YOU ARRIVE AT PETRA FIRST THING IN THE MORNING, HEAD STRAIGHT TO THE MONASTERY – A LONG WALK, BUT WORTH IT AS YOU WILL HAVE THE WHOLE PLACE TO YOURSELF.

02
SUMMER

EXPERIENCE THIS

IT'S JUNE IN SWEDISH LAPLAND AND THE TIME IS 2300.
FINISH SUPPER AT AN AWARD-WINNING RESTAURANT
BEFORE HITTING THE SLOPES AGAIN, THE SUN STILL VISIBLE
OVER THE HORIZON. WELCOME TO RIKSGRÄNSEN.

EXPERIENCE THIS

EXPLORE THE COVES OF THE BEAUTIFUL MADDALENA ISLANDS MARINE PARK BY BOAT, SNORKELLING IN THE CRYSTAL CLEAR WATER AND ENJOYING A PICNIC LUNCH ON A DESERTED BEACH. IT COULD BE THE CARIBBEAN.

SARDINIA

COSTA SMERALDA

Costa Smeralda

MUST SEE The panoramic view from the top of Monte Mora » The extraordinary rock formations of Capo Testa » The pink sand beaches of the Maddalena Islands, created from ground-up coral MUST DO Head

to the mountainous interior of the island, and see the *nuraghes* – impressive stone towers built thousands of years ago » Dive some of the clearest waters in the Med » Sip *prosecco* at a terrace bar in Porto

Cervo and watch the billionaires and their arm-candy go by RESTAURANTS/BARS La Gritta, in Palau, has lovely views over the Maddalena Archipelago and serves superb seafood with Sardinian wines (Località Porto

Faro, +39 (0)789 708 045) SOUVENIRS An invitation on to a mega-yacht for next year BOOKS TO PACK *Sea and Sardinia* by D H Lawrence DON'T FORGET... Your entourage

PRICE

BEST FOR… MESSING AROUND IN BOATS (OR SUPER-YACHTS)

» Back in the early 1960's, the Aga Khan began to develop a stretch of Sardinia's idyllic north-eastern coast into the exclusive summer playground now known as the 'Costa Smeralda' (Emerald Coast). The antithesis of the Costa del Sol, planning restrictions for the development could be summarised as: luxury villa – yes; multi-storey concrete hotel – *no grazie*. As a result, what was once one of the most beautiful stretches of coastline in the Mediterranean is still, for the most part, exactly that: rugged granite headlands that shelter dozens of secluded coves, fringed with sandy beaches and famously translucent, turquoise-green waters (hence the Smeralda). The latter provide excellent conditions for every conceivable watersport, including good snorkelling and scuba diving around the islands of the nearby Archipelago della Maddalena, where Garibaldi lived out his days. Porto Cervo, the 'capital' of this pleasure-kingdom, has a marina packed with sleek yachts, and car-free streets packed with restaurants, bars and stylish boutiques. Just a short distance inland, however, is another world entirely – a rustic landscape of small villages and pine-covered hills that is well worth exploring.

TAKE ME THERE
thebigshortbreak.co.uk
+44 (0)20 7978 7333

COSTA SMERALDA

✈ 2.5 HRS FROM UK

🧳 4 DAYS
2 DAYS OFF WORK

☀ JUN 17°/23°; JUL 20°/27°
AUG 20°/27°

DAY 1 Fly to Olbia in the north of Sardinia, pick up hire car and drive to hotel of choice » Afternoon at leisure to relax on the beach and swim in the sea » Overnight at the Hotel Pitrizza or La Coluccia

DAY 2 Rent a boat for the day to explore the beautiful Maddalena Islands. The water quality here is some of the best in the Mediterranean, and you can go diving on the wrecks of old Roman cargo ships

DAY 3 Day at leisure to relax, enjoy watersports (Sardinia is particularly good for sailing and kite-surfing) or venture inland to explore the island » In the evening, head into Porto Cervo to check out the none-too-subtle display of wealth as the mega-yachts jockey for position in the harbour

DAY 4 Morning at leisure before transfer back to Olbia for return flight home

COSTA SMERALDA

HOTEL PITRIZZA

A secluded, five-star hotel overlooking a sheltered bay on Sardinia's unspoilt Costa Smeralda. *(Opening pages; this page, bottom; far page, middle)*

CHARACTER Luxury beach hotel
ROOMS 55 **FEATURES** Grass-roofed villas; private sandy beach; natural seawater pool carved out of the rock; watersports; boat trips; spa; restaurant; bar; concierge; babysitting service; tours and excursions arranged; tennis and championship golf course nearby
LOCATION Liscia di Vacca Bay, two miles from Porto Cervo

LA COLUCCIA

A strikingly modern design hotel set in a secluded position on the Coluccia peninsula on the north coast of Sardinia, a short distance from the Costa Smeralda itself. *(This page, top; far page, top left)*

CHARACTER Beach retreat **ROOMS** 45
FEATURES Bold, contemporary design; large swimming pool; sandy beach; boat rental; watersports; gym; beauty centre; restaurant with sea view terrace; bar
LOCATION Conca Verde

ADDITIONAL ACCOMMODATION

HOTEL ROMAZZINO
(NEAR PORTO CERVO)

TAKE ME THERE

thebigshortbreak.co.uk
+44 (0)20 7978 7333

PS THE MAIN COAST ROAD CAN RESEMBLE A BIG CAR PARK DURING SUMMER (ALBEIT ONE JEREMY CLARKSON WOULD DROOL OVER), SO IF YOU HAVE TO DRIVE, DO SO EARLY MORNING OR LATE EVENING.

EXPERIENCE THIS »

A 'STAR BED EXPEDITION' AT LOISABA IS A MUST.
VENTURE OUT INTO THE BUSH BY HORSE, CAMEL,
OR 4WD AND ENJOY A FAMILY SLEEP-OUT ON
RAISED WOODEN PLATFORMS UNDER THE STARS.

MUST SEE The beautiful
landscapes of the
Meru National Park »
Panoramic views
towards Mount Kenya
from the Laikipia
plateau » Your children
learning bushcraft from
tribal warriors » Baby
elephants at the David

Sheldrick Wildlife Trust
MUST DO A guided
horse ride or camel
trek in the bush » Visit
a Tharaka tribal village
in Meru National Park
» Join in traditional
Samburu or Masai
dancing in the evenings
RESTAURANTS/BARS n/a

SOUVENIRS Masai
beadwork bracelets »
A pair of 'thousand
milers' – sandals made
from old car tires – in
which you can reputedly
walk twice as far as the
Proclaimers BOOK TO
PACK Born Free by Joy
Adamson (kids) » The

Flame Trees of Thika:
Memories of an African
Childhood by Elspeth
Huxley (adults) DON'T
FORGET... Something
to give to the local
children when visiting
their school
PRICE ■ ■ ■ ■ ■

BEST FOR… YOUNG ATTENBOROUGHS » *"In the jungle, the mighty jungle, the lion sleeps tonight…"* Except that it doesn't because, like other members of the cat family, lions are nocturnal and are probably busy hunting at night. Nor do they tend to inhabit jungles, preferring open savannah and scrubland. These are the kinds of smart alec things your kids will be able to tell you after a safari in Kenya. From family-friendly lodges in the Meru National Park or the Laikipia region, children can see warthog, giraffe, lion, elephant and all the other animals they're familiar with in cartoon form from *The Lion King* (though please explain that the animals can't sing in real life). Their days can be spent identifying animal tracks (and dung), making bows and arrows, fishing, horse riding, camel trekking or stalking large beasts across the plains in the company of Samburu or Masai warriors. Visits to local villages will open their eyes to a different way of life where tribal people still lead simple, traditional lives without PlayStation. Meanwhile, parents can enjoy the magnificent scenery or a relaxing massage, safe in the knowledge that their kids are having the time of their lives. Family holiday in Africa? *Hakuna matata.*

TAKE ME THERE
thebigshortbreak.co.uk
+44 (0)20 7978 7333

KENYA KIDS' SAFARI

✈ 8 HRS FROM UK
1 HR TRANSFER

💼 6 DAYS
4 DAYS OFF WORK

☀ JUN 12°/23°; JUL 11°/22°; AUG 11°/22°

DAY 1 Arrive Nairobi after overnight flight and connect by light aircraft to Meru National Park » Lunch at lodge » Relaxing massages for mum and dad » Evening game drive » Overnight at Elsa's Kopje

DAY 2 Guided game drive in the early morning, with bush breakfast » Afternoon to swim and relax » Night drive to look for nocturnal game

DAY 3 Day trip to go fishing on the Tana River and visit a Tharaka tribal village » Return for supper at the lodge

DAY 4 Morning transfer to airstrip for flight to Loisaba » Afternoon to swim and relax » Evening game drive » Barbecue supper

DAY 5 Optional morning bush walk with well-qualified Samburu or Laikipiak Masai scouts » Afternoon for mountain biking, horse riding or camel trekking » Sleep out on 'star beds' under equatorial skies

DAY 6 Early morning game drive » Visit to local school » Lunch at the lodge » Transfer back to Nairobi for overnight return flight home

ADD-ONS Optional extra days on the Kenyan coast

KENYA KIDS' SAFARI

ELSA'S KOPJE

A luxury safari lodge situated in the wilderness of Meru National Park and named after Elsa – the lioness made famous by George and Joy Adamson in *Born Free*. *(This page, top; far page, middle)*

CHARACTER Safari lodge **ROOMS** 9 stone and thatch cottages, including Elsa's Private House – a double cottage ideal for families, set slightly apart from the rest of the lodge with its own swimming pool **FEATURES** Game drives (including night drives); guided walks; bush meals; swimming pool; fishing on Tana River; visits to tribal village; massages; Italian food; children's menus and childminders **LOCATION** Meru National Park, north-eastern Kenya

LOISABA

Perched high on the edge of the Laikipia plateau, Loisaba is a 61,000-acre private reserve and working cattle ranch which offers excellent game viewing and a wide range of other activities. *(Previous page)*

CHARACTER Safari lodge **ROOMS** 19 (including the separate Loisaba Cottage and Loisaba House, which are ideal for families) **FEATURES** Panoramic views; game drives; bush walks; horse riding; camel trekking; guiding by local Samburu and Masai warriors; mountain biking; river rafting (seasonal); hot-air ballooning; sleep-outs on 'star beds'; swimming pool; tennis; croquet; boules; spa treatments and massages; children's menus and childminders **LOCATION** Borders of Laikipia and Northern Frontier districts

ADDITIONAL ACCOMMODATION

BORANA – WHERE 'PRIDE ROCK' FROM *THE LION KING* IS LOCATED

TAKE ME THERE

thebigshortbreak.co.uk
+44 (0)20 7978 7333

P.S. BOOK THE FAMILY COTTAGES AT ELSA'S KOPJE OR LOISABA FOR PRIVACY, DEDICATED STAFF AND PRIVATE SWIMMING POOLS. THE HONEYMOON COUPLES WILL THANK YOU FOR IT.

EXPERIENCE THIS »

ICELAND OFFERS SOME OF THE WORLD'S FRESHEST SEAFOOD, BUT ALSO THE LEAST FRESH: THE TASTE OF *HÁKARL* – SHARK MEAT THAT HAS BEEN BURIED IN SAND FOR SEVERAL MONTHS – CAN ONLY BE DESCRIBED AS UNIQUE. WASH IT DOWN WITH A SHOT OF *BRENNIVÍN* (POTATO SCHNAPPS FLAVOURED WITH CARAWAY).

ICELAND

Snæfellsnes Peninsula
Reykjavik

MUST SEE Mt Snæfells, as featured in Jules Verne's *Journey to the Centre of the Earth* » The rift between tectonic plates at Thingvellir – one of the very few places where you can actually see the continental divide

MUST DO Snowmobile on a glacier » Watch for seals along the beach at Búðir » Party the night away in Reykjavik RESTAURANTS/BARS Besides local 'delicacies' such as pickled rams' testicles and boiled puffin (not recommended),

Reykjavik has some first-class restaurants Try Sólon, a lively bistro-bar-nightclub (Bankastræti 7a, 101 Reykjavik, +562 3232) SOUVENIRS A traditional Icelandic woollen jumper » *Takk* by Sigur Rós, the music

from the BBC's *Planet Earth* BOOK TO PACK *Independent People* by Halldór Laxness DONT FORGET... Swimming trunks/bikini for a relaxing soak in the Blue Lagoon PRICE ■ ■ □ □ □

BEST FOR… OUTDOOR TYPES » Raw nature is what Iceland is all about. Geologically speaking, it is the world's youngest country (and still very much a work in progress). It is also one of the emptiest – with fewer than 300,000 people in an area roughly the size of Ireland – and the least polluted, since the country meets most of its energy needs from natural geothermal power. As a result, pristine landscapes of fjord, mountain, glacier, and moss-covered lava field still dominate most of the island. Snæfellsnes is one such area – a starkly beautiful peninsula jutting into the North Atlantic on Iceland's western coast. Closely connected with the Norse *Sagas*, this region was also the birthplace of Leif Eiríksson, the first European to reach America, some 500 years before Columbus. In the long summer days, when the sun hardly sets, there are plenty of outdoor activities to choose from: fishing for sea trout or river salmon, horse riding, sea kayaking, whale-watching, hiking or snowmobiling on the glacier-topped volcano that dominates the tip of the peninsula – and plenty of daylight hours in which to enjoy them. On the way to or from Snæfellsnes, spend 24 hours in Reykjavik and sample the legendary nightlife of the world's most northerly capital.

TAKE ME THERE
thebigshortbreak.co.uk
+44 (0)20 7978 7333

ICELANDIC WILDERNESS ADVENTURE

✈ 3 HRS FROM UK

🧳 4 DAYS
2 DAYS OFF WORK

☀ JUN 7°/12°; JUL 9°/14°
AUG 8°/14°

DAY 1 Iceland straddles two continental plates so when you land at Keflavik airport you are technically in North America » Drive to the Blue Lagoon for a swim in the warm, mineral-rich water » Evening to enjoy Reykjavik's renowned nightlife

DAY 2 Scenic drive to the Snæfellsnes Peninsula » Go for a walk along the coast » Afternoon to go sea or river-fishing, ride an Icelandic horse (unique in having five gaits instead of the usual four), or snowmobile on the Snæfellsjökull glacier

DAY 3 Day to enjoy more activities from Snæfellsnes: drive to Stykkishólmur and take a boat trip (or go sea kayaking) through the thousands of islets in Breiðafjörður » Alternatively, go whale-watching in Faxaflói Bay (Iceland is one of the world's best whale-watching locations – species include minke, humpback and the occasional blue whale)

DAY 4 Drive back to Reykjavik » Take a tour to see Thingvellir National Park, the impressive double-tiered waterfall at Gullfoss, the geysers at Geysir (after which all others are named) and the Kerið volcanic crater » Return flight home

ICELANDIC WILDERNESS ADVENTURE

HÓTEL BÚÐIR

Búðir is an escapist's paradise –
a remote, oceanfront property
in beautiful, peaceful surroundings.
(This page, top)

CHARACTER Boutique country-house
hotel **ROOMS** 28 **FEATURES** Gastronomic
restaurant with views of ice-capped
Mt Snæfells; snowmobile trips; boat
trips; river and sea-fishing; horse riding;
hiking; whale-watching **LOCATION**
Snæfellsnes Peninsula

101 HOTEL

Iceland's first design hotel, the 101
has stylish Nordic interiors and a
prime location close to Reykjavik's
nocturnal action. *(This page, bottom)*

CHARACTER Boutique design hotel
ROOMS 38 **FEATURES** Light, spacious
rooms; billiards room; small gym;
mini-spa with steam bath and plunge
pool; popular bar-restaurant; easy
walking distance to shops, cafés and
clubs **LOCATION** Downtown Reykjavik

HOTEL NORDICA

A large, modern hotel situated
a short distance from downtown
Reykjavik and boasting the finest
facilities in the city.

CHARACTER Contemporary **ROOMS**
252 **FEATURES** Comprehensive spa;
good restaurant; bar; executive
lounge with panoramic city views
LOCATION Reykjavik

TAKE ME THERE

thebigshortbreak.co.uk
+44 (0)20 7978 7333

PS ICELAND IS WARMER
THAN ITS NAME SUGGESTS.
LIKE BRITAIN, IT BENEFITS
FROM THE GULF STREAM,
SO IS NOT NEARLY AS ICY AS
ITS MISLEADINGLY-NAMED
NEIGHBOUR, GREENLAND.

EXPERIENCE THIS »

SIT AT A VIP TABLE ON PERHAPS THE COOLEST NIGHTCLUB TERRACE IN THE WORLD, AT CAVO PARADISO ON MYKONOS, AND LISTEN TO THE WORLD'S TOP DJS PLAYING LIVE.

CYCLADES ISLANDS

PERIVOLAS

One of the most famous hotels in Greece, Perivolas consists of classic, white-washed houses built into the volcanic cliffs high above the blue Aegean. *(This page, top; far page, middle right)*

CHARACTER Boutique Mediterranean chic **ROOMS** 19 **FEATURES** Beautifully converted traditional cave dwellings with terraces overlooking Santorini's caldera; stunning swimming pool with great views and poolside café-bar; landscaped gardens; gym; outdoor Jacuzzi; sauna; steam room; massage and spa treatments **LOCATION** Above the village of Oía, on Santorini

BELVEDERE

An ultra-stylish, five-star hotel designed in the style of a Cycladic village and set high on a hill which overlooks Mykonos Town (Hora). *(Far page, middle)*

CHARACTER Boutique Mediterranean chic **ROOMS** 45 **FEATURES** Swimming pool; gym; steam room; massages; concierge; two restaurants (including Nobu in summer months); Sunset Sake Bar with great views; walking distance to Mykonos town centre **LOCATION** Mykonos

ADDITIONAL ACCOMMODATION
IKIES (SANTORINI)
KIVOTOS CLUBHOTEL (MYKONOS)

TAKE ME THERE
thebigshortbreak.co.uk
+44 (0)20 7978 7333

PS TAKE A BOAT FROM HORA TO SEE THE RUINS ON DELOS, INCLUDING THE TEMPLE OF DIONYSUS, ANCIENT GREEK GOD OF WINE AND REVELRY – A SUITABLE PILGRIMAGE FOR TODAY'S HEDONISTS.

EXPERIENCE THIS »

FEW PLACES ON EARTH CONJURE UP SUCH A SENSE
OF SPACE AS THE NAMIB DESERT. THE VIEWS ARE EPIC
IN SCALE – AGORAPHOBICS BE WARNED.

MUST SEE The stunning desert landscapes of the Namib » The skeletal remains of long-dead camelthorn trees in the 'Dead Vlei', near Sossusvlei » Ostriches running across the plains **MUST DO** Climb the world's tallest sand dunes at Sossusvlei for a view over the 'sand sea' » Lie in bed at Wolwedans and watch dawn break on the Nubib Mountains » Try to solve the mystery of the 'fairy circles' that pepper the plains on NamibRand Nature Reserve **RESTAURANTS/BARS** In Windhoek, try Nice – a stylish new restaurant and bar serving classic Namibian and international cuisine (No 2 Mozart Street, Windhoek, +264 61 300 710) **SOUVENIRS** Adopt a fairy circle – the money raised goes to a conservation foundation **BOOK TO PACK** *The Other Side of Silence* by André Brink **DON'T FORGET...** Spare memory sticks for your digital camera – you *will* use them **PRICE** ■■■■□

BEST FOR… PHOTOGRAPHERS » In a country famed for its spectacular scenery, the ancient Namib Desert from which Namibia takes its name is undoubtedly the star attraction. This 80 million-year-old wilderness — the oldest desert in the world — contains unique flora and fauna, but is above all a visual paradise. The giant red dunes of Sossusvlei, framed against a blue sky, are perhaps the most impressive sight of all — especially at sunrise or sunset, when the colours are at their most intense. On the rare occasions when the *vlei* fills with water, the resulting turquoise lake makes the view from the top of one of the 300-metre-tall dunes even more surreal. Not far from Sossusvlei lie the broad, open expanses of the NamibRand Nature Reserve. Virtually all facets of the Namib are represented here, from mountains to dune belts and grassy plains dotted with granite *kopjes*. This is the perfect place to unwind, experience the peace, space and grandeur of the desert, and discover the remarkable adaptations of indigenous plants and creatures — from the *!nara* melon (the *!* indicates a 'click' in the Nama language) to the fog-harvesting *tok-tokkie* beetle (ask your guide) and the graceful oryx — all surrounded by some of the most breathtaking scenery in Namibia, if not the whole of Africa.

TAKE ME THERE
thebigshortbreak.co.uk
+44 (0)20 7978 7333

NAMIB DESERT SAFARI

✈ 10.5 HRS FROM UK
1 HR TRANSFER

🧳 5 DAYS
3 DAYS OFF WORK

☀ JUN 10°/25°: JUL 9°/25°
AUG 11°/30°

DAY 1 Arrive at Windhoek after overnight flight from London » Connect with 'dune hopper' flight to the Sossusvlei area » Evening excursion to the towering dunes at Sossusvlei and the nearby Sesriem Canyon

DAY 2 Transfer to the NamibRand Nature Reserve » Lunch and siesta » Scenic game drive or nature walk in the reserve » Sundowner drinks amid the red dunes, with wonderful views » Candle-lit supper and star-gazing

DAY 3 Watch dawn break from your bed and see sand-grouse flying in to drink at a waterhole » Full day's safari with picnic lunch in the wild » Return to camp/lodge for supper and drinks round the campfire

DAY 4 Day-trip to the Fish River Canyon or Lüderitz (by scenic flight) or just relax at NamibRand, enjoying the peace of the desert and the ever-changing colours of the landscapes

DAY 5 Dawn hot-air balloon flight over the desert » Champagne breakfast on landing » Rest of morning to relax or go on a game drive/walk » Afternoon transfer back to Windhoek for flight home, arriving next morning

NAMIB DESERT
SAFARI

SOSSUSVLEI WILDERNESS CAMP
A very comfortable mountainside
lodge, located on a private reserve
within easy driving distance of the
magnificent Sossusvlei dunes.
(This page, bottom)

CHARACTER Desert safari lodge
ROOMS 9 **FEATURES** Thatched chalets
with private plunge pools; panoramic
views over the desert plains; bar;
outdoor dining under the stars;
4WD excursions to Sossusvlei; nature
drives and walks; hot-air ballooning
LOCATION Near Sesriem

WOLWEDANS
A collection of small, stylish safari
camps scattered around the expansive
NamibRand Nature Reserve. Choose
between the rustic Dune Camp,
the more elaborate Dunes Lodge,
the secluded Private Camp and the
exclusive new Boulders Camp –
or any combination of these.
(Previous page; far page, bottom)

CHARACTER Desert safari camps
ROOMS Dune Camp 6; Dunes Lodge
10; Private Camp 2; Boulders Camp 4
FEATURES Variety of accommodation
options to suit preferred levels of
comfort; game drives and nature walks;
hot-air ballooning; hiking; scenic flights
to Diamond Coast; day trips to Fish River
Canyon and Lüderitz; sundowner drinks
on the dunes; excellent food and wine
LOCATION NamibRand Nature Reserve

TAKE ME THERE
thebigshortbreak.co.uk
+44 (0)20 7978 7333

P.S THE CLEAR, DRY AIR AND LACK OF LIGHT POLLUTION IN THE NAMIB MAKE FOR AMAZING NIGHT SKIES. THE CANOPY OF STARS STRETCHES RIGHT DOWN TO THE HORIZON.

EXPERIENCE THIS »

LEARNING TO SURF – EVEN WITH THE BEST INSTRUCTION –
CAN BE FRUSTRATING, BUT THE FIRST TIME YOU MANAGE TO
STAND UP AND RIDE A WAVE IS A MOMENT TO REMEMBER.
AS WITH MOST THINGS, YOUNGSTERS GET THE HANG OF
IT FAR QUICKER.

SURF MONTE VELHO

MONTE VELHO NATURE RESORT

A small, eco-friendly hotel in the peaceful surroundings of the Costa Vicentina Natural Park on the southwest coast of Portugal, just minutes away from Europe's best surfing beaches. *(This page, top; far page, top left)*

CHARACTER Farmhouse **ROOMS** 9
FEATURES Rural tranquillity (rooms with outdoor hammocks but no TVs); breakfast room with scenic terrace; surf school; trekking and donkey rides in the reserve; massages and yoga on request; sailing and windsurfing nearby
LOCATION Carrapateira

POUSADA DO INFANTE

A cliff-top hotel in the historic village of Sagres, in the south-west corner of Portugal, with great views over the Atlantic Ocean.

CHARACTER Traditional **ROOMS** 51
FEATURES Good seafood restaurant; seawater swimming pool; tennis court; good surfing beaches nearby
LOCATION Sagres

TAKE ME THERE
thebigshortbreak.co.uk
+44 (0)20 7978 7333

PS DON'T STRAP THE LEASH OF YOUR SURFBOARD AROUND YOUR ANKLE UNTIL YOU REACH THE WATER – YOU MIGHT TRIP OVER THE CORD ON THE BEACH, WHICH WOULD BE, LIKE, BLEAK DUDE.

EXPERIENCE THIS »

THE FINAL STRETCHES TO THE SUMMIT ARE HARD
WORK BUT WORTH EVERY HEAVY FOOTSTEP FOR
THE SENSE OF ACHIEVEMENT YOU GET AT THE TOP.
IF YOU'RE LUCKY ENOUGH TO HAVE A CLEAR NIGHT,
CLIMBING BY MOONLIGHT IS A BEAUTIFUL EXPERIENCE.

CLIMB MONT BLANC

HAMEAU ALBERT 1ER
Chamonix's top hotel, the Hameau Albert 1er offers a blend of contemporary and traditional luxury, with many rooms enjoying views of Mont Blanc. *(Far page, bottom left)*

CHARACTER Five-star chalet **ROOMS** 36 **FEATURES** Indoor and outdoor swimming pools; spa; sauna; *hammam*; gym and climbing wall; two excellent restaurants; 20,000-bottle wine cellar **LOCATION** Chamonix

MOUNTAIN HUTS
The simple mountain huts in the high Alps offer basic accommodation for mountaineers. Short on creature comforts, but after a long day on the mountain they are as welcome as any five-star hotel.

CHARACTER Mountain refuge **ROOMS** Bunk beds in dormitories **FEATURES** A roof over your head; warmth; wholesome food; basic bathroom facilities **LOCATION** High altitude Alps

TAKE ME THERE
thebigshortbreak.co.uk
+44 (0)20 7978 7333

PS HOWEVER FIT YOU MAY BE, DON'T BE TEMPTED TO FOREGO THE TWO DAYS OF ACCLIMATISATION – THIS COULD WELL RESULT IN ALTITUDE SICKNESS AND FAILURE TO REACH THE SUMMIT.

EXPERIENCE THIS »

GO TO LIVINGSTONE ISLAND, PERCHED IN MID-STREAM AT THE VERY CREST OF THE VICTORIA FALLS. FOR AN UNFORGETTABLE CLOSE ENCOUNTER WITH ONE OF THE NATURAL WONDERS OF THE WORLD, YOU CAN SWIM IN ROCK POOLS JUST FEET FROM THE EDGE.

MUST SEE Sunrise over the Zambezi on a dawn canoe safari » Elephants crossing the Luangwa River and herds of buffalo up to 1,000 strong » Nocturnal wildlife on a night game drive » Animals coming to feed and drink at Buca Buca lagoon in the South Luangwa National Park MUST DO A scenic microlight flight over Vic Falls » A walking safari in the South Luangwa » Cast for tiger fish on the Chongwe River

RESTAURANTS/BARS n/a SOUVENIRS Hand-painted cushion covers, table cloths or bedspreads from Tribal Textiles in the South Luangwa » A video of yourself bungee jumping from the Victoria Falls Bridge

BOOK TO PACK North of South: An African Journey by Shiva Naipaul DON'T FORGET... Appropriate footwear for walking safaris » A waterproof bag to protect your camera from the spray at Vic Falls PRICE ▪▪▪▪▪

BEST FOR… WALKING AND RIVER SAFARIS » Known by the much more apt name of Mosi-oa-Tunya ('the smoke that thunders') to the local Kololo tribe who first showed them to David Livingstone, the Victoria Falls are one of the greatest sights in nature. When the Zambezi is in flood, the spray from the mile-wide falls as they plunge into the gorge below can be seen from miles away. The falls are a focus for all kinds of hair-raising activities, from white-water rafting to bungee jumping and the original gorge swing. Upstream, more sedate pastimes include canoe safaris and picnics on river islands. Zambia is also renowned as one of the best game viewing destinations in Africa. The Lower Zambezi region is famous for its large herds of elephant and a sizeable population of the rare African wild dog, while the Luangwa Valley, which marks the southern end of the Great Rift Valley, is one of the continent's great unspoilt wildernesses. Its ox-bow lagoons, plains and woodlands host huge concentrations of game – including leopard, lion, giraffe, hippo and over 400 species of birds. From learning about the lives of termites to tracking buffalo and discovering unusual plants such as the sausage tree, a walking safari here represents a wildlife experience second to none.

TAKE ME THERE
thebigshortbreak.co.uk
+44 (0)20 7978 7333

ZAMBIA: VIC FALLS & WALKING SAFARIS

✈ 10 HRS TO LUSAKA OR 11 HRS TO JOHANNESBURG 0.5-1.5 HRS TRANSFER

💼 7 DAYS 5 DAYS OFF WORK

☀ JUN 8°/27°; JUL 7°/26° AUG 11°/29°

DAY 1 Arrive Johannesburg or Lusaka after overnight flight » Onward flight to Livingstone and transfer to Tongabezi » Canoe safari on the Zambezi » Evening river cruise with sundowner drinks

DAY 2 Wake to the sound of hippos wallowing nearby » Day trip to Victoria Falls, with scenic flight or other activities in Batoka Gorge below the falls

DAY 3 Fly to Mfuwe and transfer to Tena Tena in the South Luangwa National Park » Evening game drive » Overnight at Tena Tena

DAY 4 Wake up drum for dawn departure on an expertly guided walking safari » See the spectacular yellow-billed stork colony

DAY 5 Fly to the Lower Zambezi National Park » Siesta and swim in the pool » Night game drive » Overnight Chongwe House

DAY 6 Canoe safari on the Zambezi » See crocodiles sunning themselves and carmine bee-eaters nesting in the riverbanks

DAY 7 Early morning flight back to Johannesburg or Lusaka to catch daylight flight back home

ZAMBIA: VIC FALLS & WALKING SAFARIS

TONGABEZI
A luxurious riverside safari lodge situated on the banks of the Zambezi, approximately 12 miles upstream from Victoria Falls.

CHARACTER Safari lodge **ROOMS** 10 at Tongabezi. Nearby Tangala House sleeps 8 (ideal for families or small groups) **FEATURES** Trips to Victoria Falls and Livingstone Island; canoeing; fishing; game drives; guided walking; birdwatching; picnic lunches; scenic flights over the falls; white-water rafting, bungee jumping and gorge swing nearby **LOCATION** Upper Zambezi River

TENA TENA
A remote, intimate safari camp in the South Luangwa National Park, with stunning views over a sweeping bend of the Luangwa River.

CHARACTER Tented safari camp **ROOMS** 5 **FEATURES** Walking safaris with some of Africa's best guides; game drives; river safaris **LOCATION** South Luangwa National Park

CHONGWE RIVER HOUSE
A uniquely designed private house located on the banks of the Chongwe River, a tributary of the Lower Zambezi. Chongwe House is booked on an exclusive basis. *(Previous page; this page, top)*

CHARACTER Designer bush home **ROOMS** 4 **FEATURES** Complete privacy; stunning views; swimming pool; game drives; walking and canoeing safaris; fishing **LOCATION** Chongwe River

ADDITIONAL ACCOMMODATION
RIVER CLUB (VICTORIA FALLS)
NSEFU (SOUTH LUANGWA)
NKWALI (SOUTH LUANGWA)

TAKE ME THERE
thebigshortbreak.co.uk
+44 (0)20 7978 7333

P9 THE SOUTH LUANGWA REGION OF ZAMBIA IS FAMED FOR ITS EXCELLENT WALKING SAFARIS, WHICH ARE LED BY HIGHLY EXPERIENCED GUIDES AND ACCOMPANIED BY ARMED SCOUTS.

EXPERIENCE THIS »

IF YOU ARE ON THE ISLAND WHEN ONE OF THE VILLAGES CELEBRATES ITS PATRON SAINT'S DAY, HEAD ALONG TO ENJOY THE FIESTA. GOZITANS KNOW HOW TO PARTY, AND THE HUGE CLAN FLAGS FLYING FROM THE ROOFTOPS ARE A GREAT SIGHT.

GO TO GOZO

KEMPINSKI SAN LAWRENZ
A five-star resort on the west coast of Gozo, with facilities including a dive centre and one of the most comprehensive spas in Europe. *(This page, top)*

CHARACTER Five-star resort **ROOMS** 122 **FEATURES** Spa specialising in Ayurvedic treatments and marine therapy; dive centre; large gardens; three outdoor pools (two for adults only, one for children) and an indoor pool; steambath; gym; two squash courts; two flood-lit tennis courts; yoga, Pilates and aqua aerobics; Maltese and Italian restaurants with outdoor terraces; café; two pool-bars; boat trips; guided mountain biking and hiking; bicycle and scooter rental **LOCATION** San Lawrenz, Gozo

FARMHOUSE-VILLAS
Alternatively, to really get away from it all, rent a farmhouse-villa with a swimming pool (and catering if required) in one of the peaceful little villages of the interior. Ideal for groups of friends.

TAKE ME THERE
thebigshortbreak.co.uk
+44 (0)20 7978 7333

PS HEAD CROSS-COUNTRY TO WIED IL-GHASRI AND YOU WILL FIND A STONE STAIRCASE DOWN TO A PRETTY AZURE INLET WITH A PEBBLE BEACH, WHICH YOU MIGHT HAVE ALL TO YOURSELVES.

EXPERIENCE THIS »

PADDLE ACROSS TO THE ISLAND OF SIPAN, BEACH YOUR KAYAK IN THE TINY HARBOUR OF SUDURAD AND EXPLORE THE ISLAND'S HISTORIC RUINS AND CHURCHES BY MOUNTAIN BIKE – THE PERFECT WAY TO SPEND A SUMMER'S DAY.

EXPERIENCE THIS »

A SUNDOWNER TRIP ON *UTAMADUNI*, THE TRADITIONAL SAILING DHOW AT MANDA BAY, IS A GREAT WAY TO SPEND AN EVENING. BETTER STILL, IF YOU GO ON AN OVERNIGHT CRUISE YOU CAN SLEEP ON DECK UNDER THE STARS.

EXPERIENCE THIS »

TASTING SOME OF FRANCE'S INFINITE VARIETY
OF CHEESES AT A COUNTRY MARKET IN A
CHARMING PROVENÇAL TOWN IS ONE OF
THE GREAT PLEASURES IN LIFE.

03
AUTUMN

EXPERIENCE THIS »

MEANDER THROUGH THE FLOODPLAINS OF THE OKAVANGO DELTA ON THE BACK OF THE WORLD'S LARGEST LAND ANIMAL FOR A UNIQUE PERSPECTIVE ON A UNIQUE ENVIRONMENT.

AT A GLANCE

OKAVANGO
DELTA SAFARI

BOTSWANA

Okavango
Delta

Gaborone

MUST SEE Some of the biggest herds of elephant in Africa » Birds such as Pel's fishing owl, African skimmers and fish eagles » Sunset over the delta » *Mthondo Mbonvo* ('Painted Penis') — one of the bull elephants at Abu Camp, so named because he lacks pigmentation on his impressive appendage **MUST DO** Paddle silently along the waterways of the Okavango in a *mokoro* canoe — a great way to see the delta's flora and fauna up close, especially birdlife » Swim with the elephants at Abu Camp (unless you prefer your bathing pachyderm-free) » Enjoy drinks round the campfire, listening to the sounds of the African night **RESTAURANTS/ BARS** n/a **SOUVENIRS** Hand woven baskets made by the Bayei and Hambkushu tribes » Carved wooden salad servers **BOOK TO PACK** *The No. 1 Ladies' Detective Agency* by Alexander McCall Smith **DON'T FORGET…** Your binoculars **PRICE** ■ ■ ■ ■ ■

BEST FOR… HONEYMOONERS » Fed by rains that fall far away in the central African tropics, the Okavango River empties itself not into a sea or lake, but into the sands of the Kalahari Desert, in landlocked Botswana. The result is the largest inland delta on Earth, which expands and contracts with the annual floods, irrigating the desert and creating a pristine wilderness of myriad lagoons, waterways and islands. The water acts as a magnet for wildlife, making the Okavango one of the world's most important wetlands and a bio-diversity hotspot. The delta is home to familiar species such as giraffe, hippo, buffalo and crocodile, as well as significant populations of rarer species like sitatunga, sable and red lechwe. Predators include lion, leopard, cheetah and the endangered African wild dog, and the birdwatching is exceptional, with over 500 regularly occurring species. Dotted around the delta, and accessible only by light aircraft, are a number of luxury safari camps from which guests can explore the natural wonders of the Okavango on land (either by 4WD, on horseback or on foot), on water (by *mokoro* – traditional dugout canoe) or even on the back of the ultimate amphibious all-terrain vehicle – an elephant.

TAKE ME THERE
thebigshortbreak.co.uk
+44 (0)20 7978 7333

OKAVANGO
DELTA SAFARI

✈ 11 HRS FROM UK
2.5 HRS TRANSFER

5 DAYS
3 DAYS OFF WORK

☀ SEP 14°/31°; OCT 16°/32°;
NOV 18°/33°

DAY 1 Arrive Johannesburg after overnight flight » Connecting flight to Botswana and onwards by light aircraft to the Okavango delta » Transfer from airstrip to safari camp » Lunch and siesta » Sundowner game drive

DAY 2 Wake to dawn over the delta » Early morning game drive, expertly guided nature walk, *mokoro* trip, horse ride or elephant safari » Brunch back at camp » Afternoon to relax » Evening game viewing » Drinks round the campfire and supper under the stars » Night drive to see nocturnal game » Fall asleep to sound of hippo grunts and distant (or sometimes not so distant) lion roars

DAYS 3 & 4 Game viewing and exploring the delta as per Day 2

DAY 5 Time for a last bit of game viewing followed by brunch and transfer to airstrip for return flights home

OKAVANGO DELTA SAFARI

VUMBURA PLAINS

Located in a large private concession in the remote far north of the Okavango delta, Vumbura Plains offers some of the best wildlife viewing in Botswana. *(This page, bottom)*

CHARACTER Safari lodge **ROOMS** 14 **FEATURES** Rooms with plunge pools and shaded verandahs; raised dining area overlooking the floodplain; bar; game viewing on land and water; walking safaris; night drives; campfires in the evenings **LOCATION** Kwedi Reserve, Okavango delta

ABU CAMP

Set in a 400,000-acre reserve in the heart of the Okavango delta, Abu Camp is the home of the original elephant-back safaris. *(This page, top)*

CHARACTER Safari lodge **ROOMS** 6 **FEATURES** Elephant-back safaris; luxurious tented rooms on raised platforms; game viewing on land and water (including night drives); nature walks; superb dining; library; bar with viewing deck over a waterhole; campfires in the evenings **LOCATION** Selinda Reserve, Okavango Delta

ADDITIONAL ACCOMMODATION

KWETSANI CAMP

TAKE ME THERE

thebigshortbreak.co.uk
+44 (0)20 7978 7333

 WEAR THE RIGHT
COLOURED CLOTHING ON
SAFARI – MUTED COLOURS
ARE BEST. BRIGHT COLOURS,
ESPECIALLY WHITE, MAKE YOU
EASY TO SPOT; DARK COLOURS
ATTRACT THE MOZZIES.

EXPERIENCE THIS »

HIRE A BICYCLE OR SCOOTER TO EXPLORE ONE OF THE MEDITERRANEAN'S MOST BEAUTIFUL ISLANDS, OR TO SEE CAPRI IN REAL STYLE, CHARTER A SPEEDBOAT FOR THE DAY.

MUST SEE Panoramic
views over the Bay of
Naples from Monte
Solaro » Villa Jovis, the
largest of Emperor
Tiberius' villas » Capri
from a scooter MUST DO
Swim in the luminous
waters of the Blue
Grotto » Walk the

Migliera pathway to the
Belvedere del Tuono
viewpoint » An evening
passeggiata through
the narrow cobbled
streets of Capri town
RESTAURANTS/BARS
Fontelina serves delicious
fresh seafood near the
impressive rock stacks

at Faraglioni – a nice
spot for a swim (Località
Faraglioni, +39 081 837
0845) SOUVENIRS A pair
of made-to-measure
Capri trousers or
sandals (ready within
the day) » Some of
Capri's famous ceramic
tiles » A bottle of the

local *limoncello* BOOK
TO PACK *The Story of
San Michele* by Axel
Munthe DON'T
FORGET… Your Jackie
Onassis sunglasses
PRICE ■■■■□

BEST FOR… ITALOPHILES » Rising dramatically from the blue waters of the Mediterranean, at the southern edge of the Bay of Naples, mountainous Capri has been a popular island retreat since Caesar Augustus first took a shine to it in 29BC. Tiberius ruled the Roman Empire from here for the last decade of his life, and the remains of his imperial villas can still be seen. More recently, Capri has been a favoured haunt for writers, artists and film stars. Even Lenin was a fan. Autumn is an ideal time to go, when the summer crowds have mostly gone and the sea has warmed up nicely. Base yourself at the immaculate Capri Palace, perched high above the sea in the village of Anacapri, and enjoy one of the best spas in Europe, Michelin-starred cuisine and genuinely stunning views. It is tempting to remain in this luxurious hilltop refuge and do nothing at all, but that would be to miss out on Capri's other pleasures: wonderful scenic walks through vineyards and orchards, boat trips around the island, swimming in secluded coves, and watching the world go by while sipping espresso in the *piazzetta* of Capri town. Alternatively, Naples, Pompeii, and the attractive towns of the Amalfi Coast are just a short hop across the water.

TAKE ME THERE
thebigshortbreak.co.uk
+44 (0)20 7978 7333

LA DOLCE VITA IN CAPRI

✈ 2.5 HRS FROM UK

🧳 5 DAYS
3 DAYS OFF WORK

☀ SEP 16°/26°; OCT 12°/22°;
NOV 9°/17°

DAY 1 Fly to Naples » Transfer to Capri by hydrofoil, private speedboat or helicopter » Settle in at the stunning Capri Palace » Dine on the terrace of L'Olivo, Capri's only Michelin-starred restaurant

DAY 2 Take the chairlift (or walk) to the top of Monte Solaro for fabulous views » Picnic lunch » Afternoon by the pool or try an algotherapy (seaweed) spa treatment » Evening ride by tractor and trailer to supper at a family-run trattoria in the olive groves

DAY 3 Walk or scooter to the Faraglioni rocks for a swim » Lunch by the water's edge » Head to Punta Carena to watch the sunset, with a bellini in hand » Join the locals for the evening *passeggiata*

DAY 4 Charter a boat and circumnavigate the island » Swim in the translucent waters of the Blue Grotto » Alternatively, visit the Villa San Michele, or take a day-trip across to Pompeii or Positano

DAY 5 Morning stroll around charming Anacapri » Transfer to Naples for flight home

ADD-ONS Extra days on the nearby island of Ischia, or on the Amalfi Coast

LA DOLCE VITA
IN CAPRI

CAPRI PALACE HOTEL & SPA

Capri's finest hotel, perched high on the slopes of Monte Solaro, has one of Europe's most renowned spas and wonderful views over the Bay of Naples or even as far as Mount Vesuvius on a clear day. *(This page, top and bottom)*

CHARACTER Five-star Mediterranean chic **ROOMS** 79 **FEATURES** 'Capri Beauty Farm' spa; large swimming pool; three restaurants (including the Michelin-starred L'Olivo); sauna; gym; bar; concierge; boutique; 50ft motorboat and 65ft sailing boat for hire **LOCATION** In the village of Anacapri

TAKE ME THERE
thebigshortbreak.co.uk
+44 (0)20 7978 7333

P.S. WAIT UNTIL THE DAY-TRIPPERS HAVE LEFT BEFORE VISITING THE BLUE GROTTO. SWIMMING IN THE INTENSE BLUE WATERS OF THIS SEA-CAVE IS A GREAT EXPERIENCE, ESPECIALLY WHEN NOBODY ELSE IS THERE.

EXPERIENCE THIS »

KAYAKING IS THE ENVIRONMENTALLY FRIENDLY WAY
TO EXPLORE THE DELTA. STOP PADDLING ONCE IN
A WHILE AND LISTEN TO THE NOISE OF THOUSANDS
OF BIRDS IN THE TREES AND REEDS AS YOU DRIFT
SILENTLY PAST.

DANUBE DELTA ADVENTURE

DELTA NATURE RESORT
A luxurious resort which makes the ideal base from which to explore one of Europe's last great wildernesses. *(Far page, middle left, top left and middle)*

CHARACTER Luxury eco-resort **ROOMS** 30 cabins **FEATURES** Nature-viewing in the delta by boat, off-road vehicle or on foot; fishing; canoeing and kayaking; regional excursions; swimming pool; massages; restaurant; bar; library; viewing tower (you can see over the border into the Ukraine) **LOCATION** On the banks of Lake Somova, Danube delta

TAKE ME THERE
thebigshortbreak.co.uk
+44 (0)20 7978 7333

P.S. LATE OCTOBER IS A GOOD TIME TO SEE THE RED-BREASTED GOOSE. ALMOST THE ENTIRE GLOBAL POPULATION OF THIS ENDANGERED SPECIES ARRIVES THEN TO SPEND THE WINTER MONTHS IN THE DELTA.

EXPERIENCE THIS »

SIPPING STRONG TURKISH COFFEE AND EATING
BAKLAVA ON THE SHORES OF THE BOSPHORUS,
WATCHING HUGE TANKERS GO BY, IS THE PERFECT
WAY TO REST WEARY LEGS BETWEEN BOUTS
OF SIGHTSEEING.

TURKISH

ISTANBUL: EAST
MEETS WEST

TURKEY

Istanbul

Ankara

MUST SEE The Hagia
Sophia – for 1,000 years
the largest church in
the world » The huge
underground cistern
of Yerebatan Sarnici (as
featured in *From Russia
With Love*) – the world's
grandest water tank »
The Blue Mosque at

dusk MUST DO Wander
through the Spice
Bazaar or the Grand
Bazaar with its 4,000-
odd shops » Take
a boat trip on the
Bosphorus » Climb
the Galata Tower for
great views of the city
RESTAURANTS/BARS

On the European
side, 360 Istanbul
(+90 212 251 1042)
has superb views » On
the Asian side, try hip
waterfront hangout
Ulus 29 (+90 212 358
2929) SOUVENIRS Take
your pick from *kilims*,
jewellery, leather

goods and genuine
Turkish delight (known
locally as *lokum*) BOOK
TO PACK *Istanbul:
Memories of a City*
by Orhan Pamuk
DON'T FORGET…
Your haggling skills
PRICE ■ ▢ ▢ ▢ ▢

BEST FOR… CULTURE VULTURES » 'If one had but a single glance to give the world, one should gaze on Istanbul.' That was the opinion of 19th-century French poet Alphonse de Lamartine, and though Turkey's capital-in-all-but-name has changed greatly since then, it remains a hugely atmospheric place, and a great destination for a cultural Big Short Break. Thanks to its strategic location on the Bosphorus, Byzantium (which became Constantinople and then, last time we checked, Istanbul) has a history on a par with Rome and is still a cultural and geographical bridge between East and West – the only city in the world to straddle two continents. As well as being packed with historical and cultural treasures, modern Istanbul has a contemporary buzz to it, symbolised by the new 'Istanbul Modern' art museum and growing numbers of hip bars, restaurants and clubs. Once you've seen some of the sights, which are far too numerous to list here, indulge in those other institutions of Turkish culture with a visit to a traditional *hammam*, a haggling contest in one of the city's sprawling bazaars, or a ferry ride to the Asian side for a Turkish coffee on Camlica Hill and panoramic views over the city.

TAKE ME THERE
thebigshortbreak.co.uk
+44 (0)20 7978 7333

ISTANBUL: EAST MEETS WEST

✈ 3.5 HRS FROM UK

🧳 3 DAYS
1 DAY OFF WORK

☀ SEP 16°/24°; OCT 13°/20°
NOV 9°/15°

DAY 1 Morning flight to Istanbul » Transfer along the shore of the Sea of Marmara to the city centre » Rest of the day to wander around the city and get your bearings » Overnight at the Four Seasons or the A'jia Hotel

DAY 2 Guided tour of the Sultanahmet district, taking in the Hagia Sofia, Topkapi Palace, Blue Mosque, hippodrome and the Yerebatan Sarnici cistern » Visit a traditional *hammam* for a thorough scrubbing

DAY 3 Visit a few more sights, such as the mosaics of the Chora Church, and go shopping in the bazaars » Alternatively, take a ferry to the Asian side or the Princes' Islands in the Sea of Marmara » Evening flight home

ISTANBUL: EAST
MEETS WEST

FOUR SEASONS ISTANBUL
Housed in an imposing building
that was once a prison, this is now
a place to come and stay voluntarily.
Boasts five-star comforts and a
superb location just yards from the
Blue Mosque and the Hagia Sophia.

CHARACTER Luxury city hotel in a
historic building ROOMS 65 FEATURES
Spa; gym; sauna; restaurant with outdoor
terrace; courtyard garden; roof terrace
with great views over the city LOCATION
Sultanahmet district

A'JIA HOTEL
A boutique, waterfront hotel housed
in a restored Ottoman-era mansion
on the Asian side of the Bosphorus.
(This page, top)

CHARACTER Boutique ROOMS 16
FEATURES Bosphorus views; restaurant
with outdoor terrace; massage service;
speedboat available for guests' use
LOCATION On the banks of the
Bosphorus in the Kanlica district.
The old city can be reached by boat
in about 30 minutes

ADDITIONAL ACCOMMODATION
ÇIRAGAN PALACE KEMPINSKI
THE SOFA HOTEL

TAKE ME THERE
thebigshortbreak.co.uk
+44 (0)20 7978 7333

PS FOR A RESPITE FROM THE HUBBUB OF THE CITY, HEAD FOR THE PEACE AND QUIET OF THE CAR-FREE PRINCES' ISLANDS IN THE SEA OF MARMARA. THE SILENCE MIGHT SEEM DEAFENING BY COMPARISON.

SOURCES DE CAUDALIE

EXPERIENCE THIS »

BATHING IN A BARREL OF RED WINE, CLEOPATRA-STYLE, MUST BE ONE OF THE FEW THINGS IN LIFE THAT FEELS EXTREMELY DECADENT BUT IS ALSO MEANT TO BE GOOD FOR YOU. SENSORY BLISS IS ENHANCED AFTERWARDS BY SIPPING ORGANIC RED VINE-LEAF TEA WHILE WRAPPED IN A THICK WHITE COTTON GOWN.

BEST FOR… A FAMILY BEACH ESCAPE » Parents have it so easy these days. Family holidays were once tricky affairs, but nowadays there are places that have got it down to a fine art and can satisfy the often conflicting generational ideas of what constitutes a good time. Cyprus is just such a place: the third largest island in the Mediterranean has a great climate in the autumn months (summer can be too hot for us pale northerners) and excellent beach hotels which are 'child-friendly' without being adult-unfriendly. For parents, there are thalasso-therapy spas, golf courses, good walking in the mountains of the interior, cliff-top monasteries, classical ruins and Byzantine churches to explore. For older children, there's the full range of watersports, tennis coaching, horse riding and so on; for younger ones, there are kids' clubs to keep them entertained; and for infants, crèches and babysitting are provided. Nor is there a shortage of options when the whole family wants to do things together: day trips by boat along the coast, island excursions, barbecues on the beach and, if a little cultural activity won't disrupt the familial harmony, the historic sights of old Paphos. Stuck for a good family holiday destination? Problem solved.

TAKE ME THERE
thebigshortbreak.co.uk
+44 (0)20 7978 7333

CYPRUS ISLAND
RETREAT

✈ 4.5 HRS FROM UK

🧳 5 DAYS
3 DAYS OFF WORK

☀ SEP 19°/30°; OCT 17°/27°
NOV 13°/23°

DAY 1 Fly to Paphos » Private transfer to hotel » Settle in at the Anassa or Almyra » Swim in the sea » Supper at one of the hotels' many restaurants

DAY 2 Day at leisure: kids' club or sailing/waterskiing/tennis lessons for children » Parents can relax on the beach or by the pool, or enjoy spa treatments » Supper of traditional meze at a local taverna

DAY 3 Drive up into the Troodos Mountains to explore ancient monasteries, tiny villages and enjoy great views of the Pentadaktylos Hills » Afternoon for watersports, tennis, spa or kids' club

DAY 4 Go walking in the Akamas Peninsula national park, or take a boat trip along the coast » Visit the mosaics and other cultural attractions of old Paphos – a UNESCO World Heritage Site

DAY 5 Morning to enjoy a last swim in the sea, game of tennis, watersports or spa treatments » Transfer back to Paphos for return flight home

CYPRUS ISLAND RETREAT

ANASSA

A five-star resort overlooking a wide bay, with one of the finest sandy beaches and the most complete range of facilities in Cyprus. *(Far page, bottom left)*

CHARACTER Luxury beach resort **ROOMS** 175 **FEATURES** Beach; thalasso-therapy spa; indoor and outdoor pools (including separate, shaded pool for kids); comprehensive watersports facilities (including scuba and sailing schools); boat rentals; floodlit tennis courts; squash; gym; table tennis; pool table; four restaurants (with children's menus); beach barbecues; excellent kids' club; babysitting service; good golf courses nearby **LOCATION** On the north-west coast, near the Akamas peninsula

ALMYRA

Sister-hotel of the Anassa, the Almyra is a stylish design hotel located on the beachfront in the historic town of Paphos. *(This page; far page, top right, top left)*

CHARACTER Beach resort **ROOMS** 158 **FEATURES** Beach; two swimming pools (including separate, shaded pool for kids); comprehensive watersports facilities; floodlit tennis court; gym; table tennis; in-room massages & beauty treatments; yoga; three restaurants (with children's menus); weekly family beach barbecues; children's playground; excellent kids' club; crèche; babysitting service; walking distance to the shops, restaurants and sights of Paphos; good golf courses nearby **LOCATION** Paphos

TAKE ME THERE

thebigshortbreak.co.uk
+44 (0)20 7978 7333

PS IN THE UNLIKELY EVENT THAT IT'S NOT BEACH WEATHER, HEAD TO THE PAPHOS AQUARIUM – WHICH HOUSES HUNDREDS OF SPECIES, AND HAS A RESTAURANT OVERLOOKING THE HARBOUR, AND CASTLE

EXPERIENCE THIS »
INTERSPERSE YOUR GAME DRIVES WITH TREATMENTS
AT AN AWARD-WINNING BUSH SPA, OR SPLASH
OUT FOR ARGUABLY THE MOST LAVISH SAFARI
ACCOMMODATION IN AFRICA.

MARRAKECH: SOUQS & SNAKE-CHARMERS

VILLA DES ORANGERS

A five-star boutique property with chic interiors, first class facilities and a prime location in the *medina* of old Marrakech. *(Far page, top left and middle)*

CHARACTER Boutique riad-hotel **ROOMS** 19 **FEATURES** Shaded courtyards; gardens; swimming pool; roof terrace; gastronomic restaurant; massage treatments; cigar cellar; concierge **LOCATION** Marrakech *medina*

JNANE TAMSNA

An immaculate property with stylish design and the atmosphere of a Moorish hacienda, surrounded by peaceful gardens. *(This page; far page, top right and bottom left)*

CHARACTER Country guesthouse **ROOMS** 24 rooms spread between five villas **FEATURES** Beautiful gardens; five swimming pools; clay tennis court; restaurant using home-grown organic produce; beauty treatments and massages **LOCATION** On a nine-acre estate in the Palmeraie – the large expanse of date palms just outside Marrakech

ADDITIONAL ACCOMMODATION

JARDINS DE LA MEDINA (*MEDINA*)
RIAD EL ARSAT (*MEDINA*)
DAR ZEMORA (PALMERAIIE)

TAKE ME THERE

thebigshortbreak.co.uk
+44 (0)20 7978 7333

EXPERIENCE THIS »
CLIMB TO THE SUMMIT OF MOUNT TEIDE IN TENERIFE,
THE HIGHEST POINT IN SPAIN, FOR SPECTACULAR VIEWS
ACROSS TO THE OTHER CANARY ISLANDS.

SPANISH ISLANDS

Santa Cruz
TENERIFE

MALLORCA
Palma

MUST SEE The scenery
of the Tramuntana
and its charming hilltop
villages such as Deià,
(Mallorca) » The
extraordinary volcanic
landscapes of El Teide
National Park (Tenerife)
MUST DO Wander the
narrow streets of

Palma's old quarter
(Mallorca) » Take
a boat trip past Los
Gigantes – giant cliffs
(Tenerife) **RESTAURANTS/
BARS** La Boveda (Passeig
Sagrera 3, +34 971 71
48 63) – Palma's top
tapas bar (Mallorca) »
Eat at one of the

seafood restaurants in
Garachico – the squid
is particularly delicious
(Tenerife) **SOUVENIRS**
A bottle of local olive oil,
or good Spanish leather
goods **BOOK TO PACK**
*Wild Olives: Life in
Majorca with Robert
Graves* by William

Graves (Mallorca) »
*The Four Voyages of
Christopher Columbus*, by
Christopher Columbus
(translated by J M
Cohen) (Tenerife)
DON'T FORGET… Your
mum – send a postcard
PRICE ■■□□□

BEST FOR… A CHILL-OUT LONG WEEKEND » Mallorca and Tenerife may conjure up images of package holidays and crowded beaches, but that's a narrow stereotype that ignores the reality of these two beautiful islands – the largest and most diverse of the Balearics and Canaries respectively. Though sun, sea and sand are obviously the major draws, both islands have far more to offer, in addition to some top-quality boutique hotels. Mallorca's rugged Tramuntana Mountains provide great walking, striking coastal scenery and charming hilltop villages, while the capital, Palma, has cultural attractions and a vibrant nightlife around its unspoilt old town. Tenerife, closer to Africa than Europe, is dominated by the Teide volcano, whose lunar landscapes are fascinating to explore. Away from the over-developed resorts of the south, the northern half of the island, known as the Isla Baja, or 'the other side of Tenerife', offers black volcanic sand beaches, picturesque towns and all kinds of activities on land, sea and air, from horse riding to surfing and paragliding. Of course, you may just prefer to relax on a sunbed with a cool drink, a good book and a view of the hills or the sea – an activity to which both islands, with more than three hundred days of sunshine a year, are ideally suited.

TAKE ME THERE
thebigshortbreak.co.uk
+44 (0)20 7978 7333

MALLORCA &
TENERIFE

✈ 2 HRS FROM UK
TO MALLORCA
4.5 HRS FROM UK
TO TENERIFE

🧳 4 DAYS
2 DAYS OFF WORK

☀ MALLORCA
SEP 18°/27°; OCT 14°/23°
NOV 10°/18°
TENERIFE
SEP 21°/28°; OCT 20°/26°
NOV 18°/24°

DAY 1 Morning flight to Mallorca/Tenerife and transfer to the Son Net/San Roque hotel » Rest of the day to relax (or swim in the natural volcanic sea-pools at the San Roque) » Supper of Mallorquin/Canarian cuisine

DAY 2 Day to explore the island: on Mallorca, go walking in the Tramuntana Mountains or explore Palma; on Tenerife, go walking or mountain biking in the Teide National Park or visit the charming towns of La Orotava and La Laguna

DAY 3 As Day 2 » Alternatively, charter a boat for the day to explore the coastline, go riding, or play golf. Tenerife also has good diving, paragliding and surfing

DAY 4 Morning to relax » Transfer back to the airport for evening flight back home

ADD-ONS On Mallorca, visit the remote Formentor peninsula (one of Winston Churchill's favourite spots); on Tenerife, take the boat to neighbouring La Gomera, from where Columbus sailed in 1492

MALLORCA & TENERIFE

GRAN HOTEL SON NEI

A five-star hotel housed in a converted 17th-century *finca*, with a peaceful rural setting in the foothills of the Tramuntana Mountains. *(This page; far page, middle left)*

CHARACTER Boutique luxury **ROOMS** 24 **FEATURES** Large swimming pool with private *cabañas* and a pool-bar; massage and beauty treatments; gym; excellent restaurant with indoor and outdoor dining; bar; 24-hour room service **LOCATION** Above the village of Puigpunyent, south-west Mallorca

HOTEL SAN ROQUE

A beautifully restored 18th-century manor house in the small coastal town of Garachico, with stylish contemporary interiors. *(Far page, bottom right)*

CHARACTER Boutique design hotel **ROOMS** 20 **FEATURES** Swimming pool; sauna; roof-top sun terrace; restaurant; bar; in-room massages; concierge; short walk to the sea; Seve Ballesteros-designed golf course nearby **LOCATION** Northwest coast of Tenerife

ADDITIONAL ACCOMMODATION

MARICEL (MALLORCA)
PORTIXOL (MALLORCA)
ABAMA (TENERIFE)

TAKE ME THERE

thebigshortbreak.co.uk
+44 (0)20 7978 7333

PS YOU CAN GET A CABLE-CAR MOST OF THE WAY UP TENERIFE'S MT TEIDE, BUT IF YOU WANT TO CLIMB RIGHT TO THE SUMMIT YOU'LL NEED TO ORGANISE A PERMIT BEFOREHAND.

OMAN DESERT ADVENTURE

EXPERIENCE THIS »

WATCH RARE GREEN, LOGGERHEAD AND HAWKSBILL
TURTLES LAYING THEIR EGGS ON A DESERTED BEACH,
OR NEW HATCHLINGS EMERGING FROM THE SAND
TO MAKE THEIR WAY DOWN TO THE INDIAN OCEAN.

MUST SEE The Friday
morning animal market
at Nizwa » Stunning
views from the slopes
of Jebel Akhdar »
Shooting stars in the
huge night skies over
the Wahiba Sands
MUST DO A camel ride
or walk in the Wahiba
Sands at sunset, when
the colours of the dunes
are particularly beautiful
» Try Omani honey
(sold on the branch)
which is some of the
best in the world »
Explore the lush palm
groves of Wadi Shab
or Wadi Tiwi

RESTAURANTS/BARS
n/a **SOUVENIRS** Mini
dishdashes for the
kids » A *kummah*
(embroidered cap
worn by Omani men)
» A *khanjar* (traditional
curved Omani dagger –
not for the kids) **BOOK
TO PACK** *Arabian Sands*
by Wilfred Thesiger
(adults); *Sindbad
the Sailor and Other
Tales from the Arabian
Nights* by N J Dawood,
illustrated by William
Harvey (kids) **DON'T
FORGET…** Your sense
of adventure
PRICE ■■■□□

BEST FOR… EXPANDING THOSE YOUNG HORIZONS »

Another half term, another parental quandary. One possible answer that will keep the kids entertained and also introduce them to another culture is a few days exploring Oman. This unspoilt corner of the Arabian Peninsula is as interesting as it is beautiful, and has a strong sense of its own history and heritage. From an excellent, child-friendly resort on the coast, a private guided safari into the desert takes in some of the best scenery that the country has to offer. Drive through the oasis villages of the interior, where traditional, rural life continues largely unchanged beneath dense clusters of date palms, and on up to the scenic Jebel Akhdar ('Green Mountain') of the Hajar range for panoramic views towards the Arabian Sea and the desert of the Rub' al-Khali or 'Empty Quarter'. Visit medieval forts that look just how castles should, and spend the night under the stars at a Bedouin camp amid the huge, rolling dunes of the Wahiba Sands. After washing off the desert dust with a swim in one of the natural pools that form in the wadis, head for the coast, where you can sail on a traditional wooden dhow accompanied by dolphins and watch rare giant turtles coming ashore at night to lay their eggs.

TAKE ME THERE
thebigshortbreak.co.uk
+44 (0)20 7978 7333

OMAN DESERT ADVENTURE

✈ 7.5 HRS FROM UK

🧳 6 DAYS
4 DAYS OFF WORK

☀ SEP 20°/31°; OCT 27°/31°
NOV 23°/30°

DAY 1 Arrive on overnight flight and transfer to Barr al Jissah Resort » Day to relax on the beach, swim and visit the Omani Heritage Village or enjoy spa treatments

DAY 2 Morning on the beach » Afternoon departure on desert safari » Drive through the Hajar Mountains to Nizwa and visit the souq, the fort (the largest on the Arabian Peninsula) and the animal market (Friday mornings only) » Overnight in Nizwa

DAY 3 Continue via Jabrin, with its impressive fort, and up into the mountains » Drive on to the Wahiba Sands » Evening camel ride before supper of typical Omani food with a Bedouin family » Sleep under the stars in the dunes

DAY 4 Breakfast at first light » Optional 'dune-bashing' » Drive to the coast, stopping to swim at a wadi

DAY 5 Early wake up to watch turtles lay their eggs on the beach » Drive back to Muscat via the ruins of Qulhat, with a walk in Wadi Tiwi, a snorkel at White Sand Beach and a swim in the freshwater Sinkhole » Overnight at Barr al Jissah

DAY 6 Morning to relax » Afternoon flight home, arriving early evening

OMAN DESERT ADVENTURE

BARR AL JISSAH RESORT & SPA

A luxurious three-hotel resort-village comprising: Al Waha (The Oasis), perfect for families; Al Bandar (The Town), also good for kids; and Al Husn (The Castle) an exclusive 'six-star' hotel. The resort occupies a private bay overlooking the Gulf of Oman, a short distance from Muscat.

CHARACTER Beach resort-village **ROOMS** 680 **FEATURES** Three private beaches; dive centre; watersports including snorkelling, kayaking and windsurfing; Oman's most comprehensive spa (including *hammam*); over a dozen restaurants and bars (including child-friendly Surf Café); Omani Heritage Village; three swimming pools; 'Lazy River'; dolphin and whale-watching trips; babysitting; kids' club; teens' club; four tennis courts; gym; nightclub **LOCATION** Near Muscat

BEDOUIN CAMP

A genuine Bedouin camp located in the Wahiba Sands – a large expanse of sand dune desert that lies between the Eastern Hajar Mountains and the Arabian Sea.

CHARACTER Genuine Bedouin **ROOMS** Guests sleep under the stars in the dunes, or in tents if it's cold **FEATURES** Beautiful desert scenery; privacy – no other guests; camel riding; traditional Omani food and coffee; 'dune-bashing' in 4WD vehicles **LOCATION** Wahiba Sands

ADDITIONAL ACCOMMODATION
AL BUSTAN PALACE

TAKE ME THERE
thebigshortbreak.co.uk
+44 (0)20 7978 7333

PS HEAD TO THE RAS AL JINZ TURTLE BEACH AT DAWN TO AVOID THE LARGER GROUPS WHO ARRIVE IN THE LATE EVENING. YOU COULD HAVE THE BEACH COMPLETELY TO YOURSELVES.

CHÂTEAU DE BAGNOLS

EXPERIENCE THIS »
A HELICOPTER FLIGHT TO NEARBY BURGUNDY,
FOLLOWED BY A CHAUFFEUR-DRIVEN TOUR OF SOME
OF THE REGION'S FINEST DOMAINES SHOULD BE
ANY WINE BUFF'S DREAM DAY.

MUST SEE A suite at the
Château de Bagnols
(preferably as its
occupant) » The
atmospheric Croix-
Rousse area of Lyon –
the old silk-weavers
district » The *cuvage*
(wine-making hall) at
Château de Bagnols

MUST DO Cycle through
the vineyards around
the château » Explore
the historic *traboules*
of Vieux Lyon » A
wine-tasting tour of
the Beaujolais or
Burgundy vineyards
RESTAURANTS/BARS
The château's Salle

des Gardes restaurant
serves Michelin-starred
cuisine in an atmospheric
banqueting hall with
an immense gothic
fireplace – reputedly
the largest in France
SOUVENIRS A cookbook
from Badiane, Lyon's
specialist cookery

bookshop » Ship home
a case of Beaujolais
or Côtes du Rhône
BOOK TO PACK *Wine
and War* by Don
and Petie Kladstrup
DON'T FORGET…
Your private jet
PRICE ■■□□□
(without the jet)

BEST FOR… BLOWING YOUR BONUS » For a weekend of no-holds-barred luxury, the Château de Bagnols, set amidst the rolling hills and vineyards of the Beaujolais region, ticks all the right boxes. The definitive luxury château-hotel, it makes the ideal base from which to enjoy the many attractions of the Rhône Valley which, despite France being the most visited country on Earth, is largely overlooked by the majority of visitors as they rush to Paris, the Alps or the Mediterranean. Less than half an hour away is Lyon, the undisputed gastronomic capital of France (and therefore, arguably, of the world). As well as the epicurean pleasures of its Michelin-starred restaurants, the city has a rich history dating back to its days as the capital of Roman Gaul. It flourished as a centre of the silk trade and was the birthplace of cinema, courtesy of the Lumière brothers, in 1895. Wander through wonderful food markets or the *traboules* (hidden alleyways) of Old Lyon – a UNESCO World Heritage Site – and sample Lyonnais specialities by one of the twin rivers. Back out in the countryside, there are the world-renowned vineyards of the Beaujolais Crus and the Burgundy region to explore, or you can just relax within the *pierre dorée* (golden stone) walls of the château and immerse yourself in the finer things in life.

TAKE ME THERE
thebigshortbreak.co.uk
+44 (0)20 7978 7333

CHÂTEAU DE BAGNOLS

✈ 1.5 HRS FROM UK

🧳 3 DAYS
0 DAYS OFF WORK

☀ SEP 12°/23°; OCT 8°/17°; NOV 4°/10°

DAY 1 Evening scheduled flight or private jet to Lyon and transfer to the Château de Bagnols » Settle into your room or suite » Apéritifs and gastronomic supper at the château's Salle des Gardes restaurant » Stagger back to your room/suite for a good night's sleep

DAY 2 Tour of the Beaujolais vineyards or private visits to some of Burgundy's best estates, with lunch at Olivier Leflaive's restaurant in Puligny Montrachet » Afternoon to visit the picturesque towns of Pérouges and Oingt » Private candle-lit dinner at the château

DAY 3 Relax at the château or go walking, cycling, horse riding or hot-air ballooning » Alternatively, spend the day in Lyon visiting the markets and other sights » Evening transfer to airport for return flight home

ADD-ONS Optional extra days to go walking in the Vercors – a beautiful outlying ripple of the Alps, just an hour south-east of Lyon

CHÂTEAU DE BAGNOLS

CHÂTEAU DE BAGNOLS
Set in the beautiful Beaujolais
countryside, Château de Bagnols,
which dates back to the 13th
century, is perhaps the finest
château-hotel in France, and
a destination in its own right.
*(Opening pages; previous page;
this page, top and bottom; far page,
top, bottom right and bottom left)*

CHARACTER Historic luxury ROOMS 21
FEATURES Entrance via a drawbridge
across a dry moat; individually designed
rooms and suites with period furnishings;
Michelin-starred Salle des Gardes
restaurant; outstanding cellar; gardens;
large terrace with scenic views for
outdoor dining; Roman-style circular
swimming pool; spa treatments and
massages; cycling and horse riding;
hot-air ballooning; visits to vineyards
of Beaujolais and Burgundy LOCATION
In the heart of the Beaujolais region,
17 miles from Lyon

ADDITIONAL ACCOMMODATION
LA COUR DES LOGES (LYON)

TAKE ME THERE
thebigshortbreak.co.uk
+44 (0)20 7978 7333

PS BEAUJOLAIS WINES ARE DISMISSED BY MANY BUT THE TEN BEAUJOLAIS CRU *DOMAINES* ARE A SERIOUS STEP UP FROM THE BEAUJOLAIS NOUVEAU IN YOUR LOCAL SUPERMARKET. ASK THE SOMMELIER FOR GUIDANCE.

EXPERIENCE THIS »

FROM THE OUTSIDE, THE UNREMARKABLE WALLS OF BOSRA'S 13TH-CENTURY ARAB FORT GIVE NO HINT OF WHAT LIES WITHIN. ONLY WHEN YOU EMERGE FROM THE DARK CORRIDORS INTO THE SUNLIGHT DOES THE PERFECTLY PRESERVED 20,000-SEAT ROMAN THEATRE – WIDELY CONSIDERED TO BE THE FINEST EXAMPLE IN THE WORLD – REVEAL ITSELF.

SYRIA

Aleppo

Damascus

MUST SEE The gilded mosaics in the Great Umayyad Mosque, the fourth holiest site in Islam » The sun setting over Palmyra » The remains of St Simeon's Basilica MUST DO Take a taxi up Jebel Qassioun, for panoramic views over Damascus » Wander the souqs of Aleppo – where even your guide might need a guide » Smoke a *narghile* (water-pipe) RESTAURANTS/BARS Neutron – Syrian food (which is universally excellent) served in the courtyard of a traditional house (Jaafar Avenue, Damascus, +544 5451) SOUVENIRS Carpets, of course, but also… inlaid wooden boxes or backgammon sets – a Damascene speciality » Olive oil soap from Aleppo, scented with laurel, mint or sandalwood BOOK TO PACK *From the Holy Mountain* by William Dalrymple DON'T FORGET… A spare bag for all your souq purchases PRICE ■■■■□

BEST FOR… HISTORY LOVERS » For those who like to immerse themselves in history, few places can compare with Syria. This fascinating country was a melting pot of different cultures and civilizations for several millennia before the term 'melting pot' was even coined. Phoenicians, Persians, Greeks, Romans, Byzantines, Arabs, Crusaders, Mamluks, Mongols, Ottomans and the French have all left their mark here. Damascus is one of several cities in the Middle East that claims to be the oldest continuously inhabited settlement in the world, and if ever a place merited the description 'timeless', this is it. In the words of Mark Twain: 'Damascus has seen all that ever occurred on earth, and still she lives.' Walk along Straight Street, where Saul had his Damascene moment and became Paul, visit the modest tomb of Saladin next to the Great Umayyad Mosque, and explore the souqs, crammed with small shops selling everything from gold jewellery to herbs, spices and colourful plastic toys. Beyond Damascus lie many more impressive sights: the classical ruins of ancient Bosra, Palmyra and Apamea, well-preserved Crusader-era castles, the atmospheric 'Dead Cities' that litter the hillsides of northwest Syria, and the evocative old city of Aleppo.

TAKE ME THERE
thebigshortbreak.co.uk
+44 (0)20 7978 7333

DAMASCUS & BEYOND

✈ 5 HRS FROM UK

🧳 7 DAYS
5 DAYS OFF WORK

☀ SEP 16°/33° · OCT 12°/27°
NOV 8°/19°

DAY 1 Arrive in Damascus after overnight flight and transfer to Beit Al Mamlouka hotel in the Old City » Explore old Damascus, including the Great Umayyad Mosque and the souqs

DAY 2 Day trip to Bosra » Wander amongst the ruins and the Roman theatre » Return to Damascus for supper at a traditional Damascene courtyard house

DAY 3 Head east across the desert to the ruined oasis-city of Palmyra » Guided tour of the ruins and the Valley of the Tombs » Watch the sunset from the hilltop fortress » Overnight at Palmyra

DAY 4 Head to the mountains » Visit Krak des Chevaliers, the finest Crusader castle » Overnight near Krak

DAY 5 Head north to Aleppo, taking in the classical ruins at Apamea and one or two 'Dead Cities' en route » Explore the Old City of Aleppo » Overnight in Jdeideh, Aleppo's Armenian district

DAY 6 Morning excursion to the Basilica of St Simeon near Aleppo » Rest of day to explore Aleppo's citadel and souqs

DAY 7 Early morning transfer to airport for flight home

DAMASCUS & BEYOND

BEIT AL MAMLOUKA

Behind its unassuming entrance lies a beautifully restored, 17th-century Damascene house, set around a central courtyard with a fountain and citrus trees. A peaceful oasis amid the hustle and bustle of old Damascus.

CHARACTER Boutique **ROOMS** 8 **FEATURES** Cool, shady courtyard; bar; roof terrace; traditional *hammam* directly opposite **LOCATION** In the Christian quarter of the Old City of Damascus

ZENOBIA CHAM PALACE

Built to house the first tourists to visit Palmyra in the early decades of the 20th century, the recently refurbished Zenobia is a small, single-storey hotel with an unrivalled position literally adjacent to the ruins.

CHARACTER Contemporary **ROOMS** 78 **FEATURES** Prime location; great views from the terrace; indoor and outdoor restaurants; bar **LOCATION** Right on the edge of the ruins at Palmyra

ADDITIONAL ACCOMMODATION

BEIT WAKIL (ALEPPO)

TAKE ME THERE

thebigshortbreak.co.uk
+44 (0)20 7978 7333

PS MANY OF THE TOP TOURIST ATTRACTIONS ARE CLOSED ON TUESDAYS – A HANGOVER FROM FRENCH COLONIAL DAYS. THE SOUQS IN DAMASCUS AND ALEPPO ARE CLOSED ON FRIDAYS.

EXPERIENCE THIS »

A PRIVATE TRIP BY WATER TAXI ALONG THE CANALS
IS AN EXCELLENT WAY TO SEE THE CITY. CROSS THE NEVA
RIVER TO THE STRELKA OR THE PETER AND PAUL FORTRESS
FOR GREAT VIEWS OF THE PASTEL-COLOURED PALACE
FAÇADES REFLECTED IN THE WATER.

ST PETERSBURG:
BALLET & BORSCHT

GRAND HOTEL EUROPE
A historic hotel occupying
a landmark building on Nevsky
Prospekt, the famous avenue
at the heart of St Petersburg.
(Far page, bottom left)

CHARACTER Grand historic **ROOMS** 301
FEATURES Excellent central location just
a few minutes' walk from the Hermitage
Museum and other cultural attractions
of St Petersburg; four restaurants offering
Russian, French, Italian and Chinese
cuisine; health club with gym, sauna,
plunge pool, massage room and spa
treatments; hair salon; florist's; selection
of boutiques; café and 24-hour bar
LOCATION Central St Petersburg

HOTEL ASTORIA
A stylish five-star hotel set on
St Isaac's Square, at the hub of
St Petersburg's city centre.

CHARACTER Contemporary **ROOMS**
213 **FEATURES** Prime central location;
many rooms with views of St Isaac's
Cathedral; restaurant serving authentic
Russian cuisine; jazz bar (open 24 hrs);
tea room; gym; sauna and steam room;
spa treatments and massages; concierge;
minutes from Hermitage and other main
sights **LOCATION** Central St Petersburg

TAKE ME THERE
thebigshortbreak.co.uk
+44 (0)20 7978 7333

 UNTIL THE RIVER
FREEZES (USUALLY IN NOVEMBER)
THE BRIDGES ACROSS THE NEVA
ARE RAISED EACH NIGHT IN THE
EARLY HOURS TO ALLOW FOR
NAVIGATION. DON'T GET STUCK
ON THE WRONG SIDE.

ST PETRI

04
WINTER

DOG-SLEDDING IN LAPLAND

EXPERIENCE THIS »
HUSKIES JUST LOVE TO RUN – IT'S AMAZING TO SEE
THEIR EXCITEMENT AS THE GUIDE PUTS THEM INTO
TEAMS, CAREFULLY BALANCED ACCORDING TO THE
STRENGTH OF EACH DOG. THE HUSKIES STRAIN AT
THEIR HARNESSES, DESPERATE TO GET OUT THERE
AND START RUNNING.

SWEDEN

Kiruna

Stockholm

MUST SEE The Northern
Lights arcing across
the night sky » An elk
(otherwise known as
a moose) » The ice
sculptures in the Ice
Hotel suites **MUST DO**
Drink vodka at the Ice
Hotel's IceBar, where
even the glasses are

made of… you know
what » Have a sauna at
one of the wilderness
cabins » Feed your
team of dogs at the
end of each day's
sledding » Drill a hole
in the thick ice of a
frozen lake or river
to fish for Arctic char

RESTAURANTS/BARS
Café Opera: a popular
bar and restaurant in
baroque surroundings.
Transforms into
a nightclub as the
evening progresses
(Operahuset,
Kungsträdgården,
Stockholm,

+46 8 676 58 07)
SOUVENIRS A reindeer
hide » Rosy cheeks
BOOK TO PACK *A Year
in Lapland: Guest of
the Reindeer Herders*
by Hugo Beach **DON'T
FORGET…** Your thermal
underwear

PRICE ■■■□□

BEST FOR… ANIMAL LOVERS » Siberian huskies, the breed of choice for dog-sledders, are perfectly adapted to their task – good-natured, energetic and able to withstand even the harshest conditions. Dog-sledding through the snowbound forests and mountains of Swedish Lapland will leave even the hardiest 'been there, done that' traveller with an indelible memory. Glide through beautiful winter landscapes, staying overnight in private log cabins and eating traditional Lapp fare such as reindeer stew with cloudberries. The dog-sledding combines with a stay at the extraordinary Ice Hotel, sculpted anew each year from the frozen waters of the Torne River. Activities here include snowshoeing, elk safaris, cross-country skiing and the chance to learn a bit about the local Lapp culture. If you are lucky, the Swedish Arctic is also one of the best places in the world to see the Northern Lights, the ethereal natural light show that occurs in the depths of winter, as shimmering bands of colour drift across the night sky. For those looking for some creature comforts and pampering before the 'rigours' of the frozen north, a night at one of Stockholm's top hotels makes a perfect prelude.

TAKE ME THERE
thebigshortbreak.co.uk
+44 (0)20 7978 7333

DOG-SLEDDING
IN LAPLAND

✈ 2.5 HRS FROM UK
1 HR TRANSFER

🧳 5 DAYS
3 DAYS OFF WORK

☀ DEC -17°/-8°; JAN -19°/-10°
FEB -18°/-8°

DAY 1 Fly to Stockholm » Stay overnight in one of the city's top hotels

DAY 2 Fly to Kiruna, deep inside the Arctic Circle, and transfer to Jukkasjärvi » Afternoon for activities at the Ice Hotel » Overnight in an Ice Room sleeping on a mattress covered with reindeer hides

DAY 3 Pick up from Ice Hotel for a full day's dog-sledding through the forests with your own team of pure-bred huskies » Overnight in a private wilderness cabin

DAY 4 Full day's dog-sledding » Overnight in a private wilderness cabin after a gourmet Swedish supper, prepared by a chef who arrives on a snowmobile

DAY 5 Dog-sled back to Jukkasjärvi » Transfer to the airport for flight home via Stockholm

ADD-ONS More nights in Stockholm » Skiing in Riksgränsen (see page 98) during March and April

DOG-SLEDDING
IN LAPLAND

ICE HOTEL
The world-famous Ice Hotel is built
from scratch each year on the banks
of the Torne River in Swedish Lapland,
130 miles north of the Arctic Circle.
Roughly 30,000 tons of snow and
4,000 tons of ice go into the structure.
(This page, bottom; far page, bottom)

CHARACTER Glorified igloo **ROOMS** 80
FEATURES Award-winning restaurant;
ice sculpting demonstrations; elk safaris;
snowmobile safaris; snowshoe trekking;
cross-country skiing **LOCATION** Jukkasjärvi

WILDERNESS CABINS
Traditional, log-built cabins with
basic but comfortable interiors
and a genuinely peaceful setting.

CHARACTER Log cabins **ROOMS** 2-4
FEATURES Cabins are equipped with
saunas, but no satellite TV or Wi-Fi
internet access, and your Blackberry
will not work **LOCATION** Middle
of nowhere

BERNS HOTEL
A historic 19th-century building with
modern, Terence Conran-designed
rooms and a great location in the
heart of Stockholm. Adjoins the
fashionable 'Berns complex' of bars
and restaurants.

CHARACTER Historic-modern blend
ROOMS 65 **FEATURES** Two restaurants;
four bars; nightclub (but guestrooms are
soundproofed to avoid disturbance);
access to spa facilities nearby **LOCATION**
Next to Berzelii Park in central Stockholm

ADDITIONAL ACCOMMODATION
GRAND HOTEL (STOCKHOLM)
NORDIC SEA (STOCKHOLM)

TAKE ME THERE
thebigshortbreak.co.uk
+44 (0)20 7978 7333

PS IT DOESN'T HAPPEN
OFTEN, BUT IF YOU DO FALL
OFF YOUR SLED, TRY TO HANG
ON TIGHT BECAUSE THE DOGS
WON'T STOP RUNNING FOR A
WHILE, AND YOU COULD END
UP WITH A LONG WALK.

EXPERIENCE THIS »

VISIT HERMANUS IN DECEMBER TO CATCH A LAST
SIGHTING OF MAJESTIC SOUTHERN RIGHT WHALES
AND THEIR NEW-BORN CALVES BEFORE THEY MIGRATE
BACK TO THE ANTARCTIC.

Cape Town · Franschhoek

AT A GLANCE

SOUTH AFRICA

CAPE TOWN &
THE WINELANDS

MUST SEE Sunset views over Cape Town from the top of Signal Hill » Characteristic Cape Dutch architecture in the winelands » Whales off the coast of Hermanus MUST DO Sea kayak around Hout Bay » A trip to Robben Island – where the anti-apartheid leaders were interned » A wine-tasting tour on horseback through the scenic winelands RESTAURANTS/BARS Tokara Restaurant, between Stellenbosch and Franschhoek, is one of the best in the winelands and has beautiful views from its outdoor terrace (+27 21 808 5959) SOUVENIRS Arts and crafts from all over Africa at the Pan African Market or Greenmarket Square in Cape Town » Ship home fine wine from Stellenbosch BOOKS TO PACK *Long Walk to Freedom: The Autobiography of Nelson Mandela* DON'T FORGET… Your appetite PRICE ■■■■□

BEST FOR… GOURMETS » With the Atlantic Ocean on one side and iconic Table Mountain as a towering backdrop, Cape Town enjoys arguably the most spectacular natural setting of any city in the world. Besides its dramatic geography, South Africa's oldest city has everything from the historic Malay quarter of Bo-Kaap to colourful markets and the beaches of Clifton and Camps Bay. If it doesn't have its 'tablecloth' of cloud, the views from the top of Table Mountain are spectacular, especially after climbing it on foot (don't worry – you can take the cable car down). Take a drive along the Cape Peninsula via False Bay, where there is good surf and the famous colony of African penguins, and then on to the Cape of Good Hope, where you can witness the power of the seas as two major ocean currents collide. Just an hour's drive from Cape Town are the beautiful Cape winelands – rolling countryside dotted with some of the finest vineyards in the 'New World'. The attractive village of Franschhoek, founded by French Huguenots in 1688, is the gastronomic capital of South Africa – the perfect place to indulge the taste-buds at some world-class restaurants. Round things off with a day or two on the coast at Hermanus, where you can sea kayak with whales, and you will have sampled the very best of the Cape.

TAKE ME THERE
thebigshortbreak.co.uk
+44 (0)20 7978 7333

CAPE TOWN &
THE WINELANDS

✈ 11 HRS FROM UK

🧳 6 DAYS
4 DAYS OFF WORK

☀ DEC 14°/24°; JAN 16°/26°
FEB 16°/26°

DAY 1 Arrive Cape Town after overnight flight » Transfer to Kensington Place » Rest of day to explore Cape Town » Wander along Long Street » Overnight at Kensington Place

DAY 2 Climb Table Mountain, with a picnic lunch on top, or explore the Cape Peninsula » Drive along the Chapman's Peak road for fantastic views of the coast

DAY 3 Morning to relax by the pool or visit the Kirstenbosch Botanical Gardens – one of the great botanical gardens of the world » Drive through the winelands to Franschhoek » Overnight at Le Quartier Français

DAY 4 Day to explore the winelands: visit some of the estates for wine tastings, or go hiking or trout fishing in the hills

DAY 5 Morning to relax or go shopping in Franschhoek » Drive via the scenic Franschhoek Pass to Hermanus » Afternoon to enjoy some of the world's best whale-watching » Overnight at Birkenhead House

DAY 6 Morning swim at Hermanus » Visit the beautiful Vergelegen wine estate at Somerset West » Continue to Cape Town airport for return flight home

CAPE TOWN &
THE WINELANDS

KENSINGTON PLACE
A stylish boutique hotel set in a leafy
residential suburb on the slopes
of Table Mountain. *(This page)*

CHARACTER Boutique **ROOMS** 8
FEATURES Great views over Cape Town
and the Atlantic Ocean; landscaped
gardens; plunge pool; terrace; cocktail
bar; dining room; concierge; activities
and day trips arranged **LOCATION**
Cape Town

LE QUARTIER FRANÇAIS
A privately-owned boutique hotel
in the village of Franschhoek in the
Cape Winelands. Consistently voted
amongst the best small hotels in
the world.

CHARACTER Country inn **ROOMS** 21
FEATURES Multi award-winning
restaurant; swimming pool; gardens;
beauty treatments; mini cinema
LOCATION Franschhoek

BIRKENHEAD HOUSE
A small, luxurious coastal retreat
perched on the cliffs overlooking
Walker Bay, just outside Hermanus
on the 'Garden Route' running east
from Cape Town. *(Opening pages:
far page, top left)*

CHARACTER Seaside hotel **ROOMS** 11
(+6 in the adjacent Birkenhead Villa)
FEATURES Dual-level swimming pool;
massage and beauty treatments;
whale-watching; cliff walks; sea kayaking;
fishing; diving; horse riding **LOCATION**
Five miles from Hermanus

ADDITIONAL ACCOMMODATION
ELLERMAN HOUSE (CAPE TOWN)

TAKE ME THERE
thebigshortbreak.co.uk
+44 (0)20 7978 7333

PS ON SUNDAY EVENINGS FROM DECEMBER TO MARCH, OUTDOOR CONCERTS ARE HELD AT SUNSET IN THE BEAUTIFUL SURROUNDINGS OF THE KIRSTENBOSCH BOTANICAL GARDENS.

EXPERIENCE THIS

IF YOU WANT TO TRY A NOVEL FORM OF TRANSPORT, TAKE THE CABLE-CAR FROM FUNCHAL TO THE HILLTOP TOWN OF MONTE, AND RIDE BACK DOWN THE STEEP STREETS IN A *CARRO DE CESTO*, A SORT OF WICKER TOBOGGAN. TWO *CARREIROS*, DRESSED IN WHITE, GUIDE THE SLED ALONG THE THREE-MILE ROUTE.

ETERNAL SPRING IN MADEIRA

CHOUPANA HILLS RESORT & SPA
A chic spa-resort with an oriental flavour, set amidst eight hectares of semi-tropical greenery with fantastic views over Funchal and the Atlantic Ocean. *(Far page, top left)*

CHARACTER Design hotel **ROOMS** 34 **FEATURES** Spa; indoor and outdoor pools; pool-bar; sauna; steam room; yoga instruction; restaurant; bar; library; shuttle service to Funchal **LOCATION** In the hills above Funchal

REID'S PALACE
Founded by Scots wine merchant William Reid over a century ago, Reid's Palace is a famous Madeiran landmark. Set overlooking the ocean, it is surrounded by ten acres of gardens that are renowned in their own right. *(Far page, bottom right)*

CHARACTER Traditional luxury **ROOMS** 163 **FEATURES** Extensive gardens; spa; sauna; steam room; gym; several restaurants; three swimming pools; tennis; good children's facilities **LOCATION** On the cliff-tops, just outside Funchal

ADDITIONAL ACCOMMODATION
QUINTA DA BELA VISTA
QUINTA JARDINS DO LAGO

TAKE ME THERE
thebigshortbreak.co.uk
+44 (0)20 7978 7333

PS AS A GENERAL RULE,
THE WEATHER CONDITIONS
IN MADEIRA CAN BE VERY
LOCALISED, SO IF IT'S CLOUDY
OR RAINING IN ONE VALLEY, GO
TO THE NEXT, WHERE IT COULD
WELL BE CLEAR AND SUNNY.

EXPERIENCE THIS

BEING IN THE WATER WITH THE ORCAS IS TOTALLY
EXHILARATING. WATCH THESE GRACEFUL PREDATORS
WORKING AS A TEAM TO CORRAL THE HERRING
SHOALS BEFORE STRIKING.

SNORKEL
WITH ORCAS

NORWAY

Narvik

Oslo

MUST SEE An orca's dorsal fin breaking the surface of the water. If you're lucky, you might also see the whales breaching (when they leap almost entirely out of the water) » Winter sunlight on the rock-faces of Stetind – the national mountain of Norway » The Northern Lights, reflected in the waters of the fjord MUST DO For the brave-hearted, take the plunge and snorkel with the orcas » A boat trip to the Ørneberget (Eagle Mountain), which plunges straight into the fjord and is home to large numbers of sea-eagles » Visit the ancient Lapp rock-carvings of animals at Dyreberget. some of which date back 9,000 years RESTAURANTS/ BARS n/a SOUVENIRS A photo of yourself in the water with the whales, or failing that, an orca soft toy BOOK TO PACK *The Vikings* by Else Roesdahl DON'T FORGET... Wind and waterproof clothing PRICE ■■■■□

BEST FOR… CLOSE ENCOUNTERS OF THE CETACEAN KIND

» Norway in winter. 150-odd miles north of the Arctic Circle. Fancy a swim in the sea? With killer whales? Crazy as it may sound, people pay good money to do exactly that. Killer whales get a bad press (the name doesn't help) but they are more properly called orcas and are not really that terrible. After all, all whales are killers, it's just that some eat krill and some eat cute, cuddly seals. The ones off the Norwegian coast come in their hundreds every year to feed on the vast shoals of herring that winter here. There are very few places in the world where orcas can be observed in such proximity and in such numbers. Taking to the water in inflatable dinghies, it is possible to watch them as they hunt in pods, driving the herring to the surface before stunning them with powerful slaps of their tails and then picking them off one by one. White-tailed sea eagles circle overhead, ready to swoop on any leftovers. This dramatic scene, framed by the snow-covered mountains of the mainland and the nearby Lofoten Islands, is truly breathtaking. The orcas' curiosity sometimes brings them right up alongside the boat, and under the right conditions you can even don a dry-suit, hop overboard and join them in their own element.

TAKE ME THERE
thebigshortbreak.co.uk
+44 (0)20 7978 7333

SNORKEL WITH ORCAS

✈ 2 HRS FROM UK
2 HRS TRANSFER

🧳 4 DAYS
2 DAYS OFF WORK

☀ DEC -5°/-1°; JAN -7 /-2°
FEB -7°/-2°

DAY 1 Fly to Narvik via Oslo and transfer to Tysfjord » Supper and slideshow presentation on orcas at Tysfjord hotel » If it's a clear night, there's a good chance of seeing the *aurora borealis* (Northern Lights)

DAY 2 Morning briefing on orca watching » Depart for orca safari in a converted trawler or inflatable dinghy » Day at sea, with expert guides seeking out the orcas and explaining their behaviour. Pilot whales, minke whales and fin whales are also sometimes seen » Lunch served on board in one of the sheltered fjords, or at a small fishing village along the coast

DAY 3 As per Day 2, or enjoy other activities, e.g. kayaking in the fjord, fishing for pollack or salmon, nature safaris in search of elk and bird species such as puffins and auks, or a visit to the ancient rock carvings at Dyreberget

DAY 4 Morning to relax or go for a walk along the shoreline before transfer back to the airport for return flights home

ADD-ONS The Ice Hotel in Sweden is only a couple of hours' drive away

SNORKEL
WITH ORCAS

TYSFJORD TURISTSENTER

A comfortable, modern hotel with a beautiful coastal setting, which also operates as a base for orca safaris and other local activities.

CHARACTER Contemporary **ROOMS** 55
FEATURES Orca safaris; fishing; kayaking; nature walks; great views of the stunning coastal scenery; restaurant; pub; rooms with wireless internet access
LOCATION Tysfjord

TAKE ME THERE

thebigshortbreak.co.uk
+44 (0)20 7978 7333

P3 KNOW YOUR ORCAS: EACH WHALE HAS ITS OWN DISTINCTIVE BLACK AND WHITE PATTERNING. THIS ENABLES THE SCIENTISTS WHO STUDY THE CREATURES TO IDENTIFY SPECIFIC INDIVIDUALS.

EXPERIENCE THIS »

EVEN THE MOST SCROOGE-LIKE CYNICS SHOULD RECALL
THE EXCITEMENT OF CHILDHOOD CHRISTMASES AND
FEEL A RENEWED SENSE OF YULETIDE CHEER WHEN FACED
WITH THE MAGICAL ATMOSPHERE OF THE TIVOLI GARDENS
CHRISTMAS MARKET.

DENMARK

Copenhagen

MUST SEE Tivoli Gardens
Christmas Market, a
delight for children and
grown-ups alike » The
changing of the guard
outside Amalienborg
Castle (every day at
noon when the royal
family is in residence)
» Denmark's national
gallery, Statens Museum
for Kunst **MUST DO** Go
ice-skating in Kongens
Nytorv, Copenhagen's
principle square » Ride
the traditional wooden
roller coaster at Tivoli
Gardens – built in 1914
and still the most
popular ride » Find
a cosy café and drink
traditional *gløgg* (a kind
of mulled wine) with
æbleskiver (spherical,
pancake-like treats)
RESTAURANTS/BARS
Noma: up-market
traditional Scandinavian
fare in a converted
warehouse on the
waterfront (Strandgade
93, +45 3296 3297)
SOUVENIRS Danish
designer goods » Royal
Copenhagen porcelain
BOOK TO PACK *Smilla's
Sense of Snow* by Peter
Høeg **DON'T FORGET…**
Your mittens
PRICE ■□□□□

BEST FOR… THE SPIRIT OF CHRISTMAS PAST » Laid-back Copenhagen is one of northern Europe's most appealing cities – with so much more to offer than just herring and Lego. Being relatively small makes it a very 'user-friendly' city to get to know, and in winter the frozen canals and frosted rooftops of the unspoilt medieval centre make it particularly atmospheric. The Danes do seasonal spirit with some style, and the run up to Christmas is one of the best times to be in Copenhagen, with the beautifully lit Christmas market at Tivoli Gardens the centrepiece of the city's festive celebrations. As a shopping destination, Copenhagen is up there with the best, selling everything from traditional tree ornaments at the markets, to avant-garde designer goods along the famous pedestrianised thoroughfare of Strøget. Long winters have taught the locals a thing or two about indoor living, and the side-streets and harbour area are packed with cosy cafés, many of which morph into lively bars and clubs in the evenings. These make perfect venues for enjoying what the Danes call *hygge* – an untranslatable state of cosy conviviality, usually attained with the help of a glass or two of probably the best beer in the world.

TAKE ME THERE
thebigshortbreak.co.uk
+44 (0)20 7978 7333

CHRISTMAS IN COPENHAGEN

✈ 2 HRS FROM UK

🧳 3 DAYS
0 DAYS OFF WORK

☀ DEC 1°/4°; JAN -2°/2°
FEB -3°/2°

DAY 1 Evening flight to Copenhagen and transfer to hotel of choice » Head out to sample the city's nightlife and take advantage of the late licensing hours

DAY 2 Breakfast of Danish pastries and coffee, followed by a full day of sightseeing, skating and Christmas festival-going (use a bicycle to get around) with a traditional *smørrebrød* at lunch time and finishing with supper in one of the restaurants at Tivoli Gardens

DAY 3 Give the credit card a good bashing on Europe's longest pedestrianised shopping street, Strøget, home to Danish designer classics such as Bodum, Bang & Olufsen, Georg Jensen, Holmegaard, and the Illum department store » Alternatively, take a day trip to Kronborg castle at Helsingør, the setting for Shakespeare's *Hamlet* » Evening flight back home

CHRISTMAS IN COPENHAGEN

HOTEL SKT PETRI

A stylish design hotel in the heart of Copenhagen, offering all the comforts of modern urban living.

CHARACTER Design hotel ROOMS 268
FEATURES East-west fusion brasserie;
café; cocktail bar with DJs on Fridays
and Saturdays; rooftop terrace and gym;
in-house yoga instructor; massage service;
concierge LOCATION Downtown
Copenhagen

HOTEL D'ANGLETERRE

Occupying an impressive mansion dating from 1755, the five-star Hotel d'Angleterre is a Copenhagen landmark, with a prime location in the heart of the city.

CHARACTER Old-world luxury ROOMS
123 FEATURES Indoor swimming pool;
spa with sauna, Turkish bath and variety
of treatments; gym; Franco-Danish
restaurant; 24-hour room service; bar;
concierge LOCATION Overlooking
Kongens Nytorv (King's Square)

ADDITIONAL ACCOMMODATION

71 NYHAVN

TAKE ME THERE

thebigshortbreak.co.uk
+44 (0)20 7978 7333

PS WHEN EATING *RISALAMANDE* (A TRADITIONAL DANISH RICE-PUDDING SERVED AT CHRISTMAS) DON'T SWALLOW THE ALMOND IF YOU SHOULD FIND IT – IT'S AKIN TO EATING THE CHRISTMAS PUDDING SIXPENCE.

EXPERIENCE THIS »

SKI TOURING ON THE RENDL PEAK ALLOWS ACCESS
TO ONE OF THE BEST OFF-PISTE ROUTES IN AUSTRIA.
IT INVOLVES A BIT OF CLIMBING, BUT A SENSATIONAL
DESCENT IN FRESH POWDER AWAITS, AND ON A
GOOD DAY THE VIEWS ARE STUNNING.

MUST SEE Fantastic
views from the top
of the Valluga peak »
Watch expert skiers
tackling the steep
couloirs (or try them
yourself) » The night
through to the early
hours… MUST DO Test
yourself against the off-
piste and moguls of
the Valluga bowl » Ski
the off-piste route
from Albonagrat down
though the trees »
Dance on tables in ski
boots at the après-ski
bars on the lower slopes
RESTAURANTS/BARS
Two popular on-piste
haunts, both with
sun terraces and
pumping music, are
the Sennhütte and
Mooserwirt. Later, hit
Kandahar nightclub
(Dorfstraße 50)
SOUVENIRS A bottle
of Jägermeister BOOK
TO PACK You really
won't need a book in
St Anton, but on the
off-chance, a good read
is *Alpine Circus: A Skier's
Exotic Adventures at
the Snowy Edge of the
World* by Michael Finkel
DON'T FORGET…
Your stamina
PRICE ■ ■ □ □ □

BEST FOR… POWDER HOUNDS AND PARTY ANIMALS »

Austria's flagship resort, St Anton has a central place in the history of alpine skiing. It was here that Hannes Schneider, the son of a local cheese-maker, pioneered the development of modern skiing techniques in the early years of the 20th century, and it was here that the first ski races were held, including the inaugural Kandahar downhill race in 1928. Today, St Anton ranks among the top few ski resorts in the world. Better suited to intermediate or advanced skiers than beginners, it is known for its challenging on-and-off-piste terrain and for the best après-ski in the Alps, drawing a young crowd that likes to ski hard and party harder. The Arlberg region, of which St Anton forms an integral part, is famous for its good snow reliability and offers over 160 miles of runs in total. On top of this, experts can hire a mountain guide and enjoy some renowned off-piste descents, snowboarders are well provided for with an excellent fun park, and there are permanent racecourses for those who want to test themselves against the clock. After all that gnarly off-piste action and phat air, enjoy *steins* or *glühwein* at any of the resort's dozens of lively bars, which stay open well into the small hours.

TAKE ME THERE
thebigshortbreak.co.uk
+44 (0)20 7978 7333

POWDER & PARTIES IN ST ANTON

✈ 2 HRS FROM UK

🧳 4 DAYS
2 DAYS OFF WORK

☀ DEC -6°/0°; JAN -8°/-1°
FEB -7°/2°

DAY 1 Morning flight to Innsbruck and transfer up to St Anton » Afternoon on the slopes » Hit the après-ski bars on your way down » Overnight at the St Antoner Hof

DAY 2 Day to ski the steeps and deeps of St Anton and the extended Arlberg ski area, including the famous Valluga bowl or the 2001 World Championship downhill course » Après-ski

DAY 3 Hire a guide and spend the day skiing off-piste trails » Boarders can head for the half-pipe, slides and jumps of the Rendl Fun Park » More après-ski (if you can handle it)

DAY 4 Morning for more skiing/snowboarding before transfer back to Innsbruck for return flight home » Collapse

POWDER & PARTIES
IN ST ANTON

ST ANTONER HOF
An intimate, five-star, family-run
hotel in the centre of St Anton. Its
interiors are a blend of traditional
Tyrolean and contemporary design.

CHARACTER Traditional alpine
ROOMS 37 **FEATURES** Rooms with
DVD players and wireless internet;
indoor swimming pool; gym; sauna;
steambath; massages; good restaurant;
bar; easy walking distance to nearest
ski lift **LOCATION** St Anton

TAKE ME THERE
thebigshortbreak.co.uk
+44 (0)20 7978 7333

PS ST ANTON'S SKIING IS CHALLENGING - BE AWARE THAT MANY OF THE RUNS THAT ARE COLOUR-CODED RED WOULD BE DEEMED BLACK RUNS IN OTHER ALPINE RESORTS.

CAFE

THE CRESTA RUN

EXPERIENCE THIS »
FEEL THE ADRENALIN RUSH AND YOUR HEART
POUNDING LIKE NEVER BEFORE AS YOU COMPLETE
YOUR FIRST DESCENT OF THE CRESTA RUN.

MUST SEE Seasoned Cresta riders showing how it's done » Horse racing or snow polo on the frozen lake » The alpine scenery of the Roseg Valley on a horse-drawn sleigh ride **MUST DO** Try not to become a member

of the Shuttlecock Club by flying off the Cresta track at this infamous turn » The 3-mile night-time sledge run to Bergun » Ski the wide open spaces of the Corvatsch Glacier **RESTAURANTS/BARS**

One of the oldest buildings in St Moritz, Chesa Veglia is an atmospheric farm-house housing three restaurants (Via Veglia 2, + 41 81 837 28 00) **SOUVENIRS** A few choice bruises and a Shuttlecock Club tie

(should you fail to heed the 'Must Do') **BOOK TO PACK** *Apparently Unharmed: Riders of the Cresta Run* by Michael diGiacomo **DON'T FORGET...** Your plus-fours – traditional garb for riding the Cresta **PRICE**

BEST FOR… ADRENALIN JUNKIES » If you are looking for something to spice up a winter's weekend, the innocuous sounding St Moritz Tobogganing Club is home to the famous Cresta Run, purveyor of adrenalin rushes to the daring and the foolhardy since 1885. A half-tube of blue ice, twisting its way for three quarters of a mile down a Swiss Alp, the Cresta is negotiated head first on a heavy sled, known rather ominously as a 'skeleton'. Riders are offered an optional 'bullshot' – a drink of vodka and hot consommé – to steady the nerves, before hurtling down the track at speeds in excess of 60mph with their noses just inches above the ice and only spiked shoes for brakes. This apparently induces a mixture of fear and exhilaration. Follow instructions and you have a good chance of reaching the finish line, but many a rider has made an airborne exit at the notorious Shuttlecock Corner. Because the descent itself is quick (the current record stands at 50.09 seconds) there is ample time to sample the many other attractions of St Moritz and the Engadine Valley, from skiing to great restaurants and nightlife. On certain weekends in January and February, there are also polo matches and the 'White Turf' horse races to watch on St Moritz's frozen lake.

TAKE ME THERE
thebigshortbreak.co.uk
+44 (0)20 7978 7333

THE CRESTA RUN

✈ 1.5 HRS FROM UK

💼 4 DAYS
1 DAY OFF WORK

☀ DEC -10°/5°; JAN -12°/3°
FEB -12°/3°

DAY 1 Evening flight to Zürich and transfer to St Moritz by car or train (or private jet direct to St Moritz) » Delicious supper of traditional Engadine cuisine at the Kulm Hotel » Overnight at the Kulm

DAY 2 Dawn briefing at the Cresta Club » Up to five descents of the famous run » Afternoon skiing » Evening rendezvous at the Sunny Bar of the Kulm – the traditional meeting place for riders of the Cresta Run

DAY 3 Watch the professional riders race the Cresta » Ski the slopes of Corvatsch and Corviglia » Evening train up to Preda for moonlit descent of the (comparatively sedate) Preda to Bergun sled run » Après-sled drink at the ice-bar and a fondue supper

DAY 4 Day of skiing, snow-shoeing, cross-country skiing, skating or curling » Alternatively, relax on the sun terrace of the Kulm and enjoy St Moritz's famous 'champagne climate' » Transfer to airport for return flight home

NB Wives of Cresta Club members may ride the course on the final day of the season. Women were barred from partaking more regularly in 1929 for health reasons, but some suspect it was because they were becoming too good

THE CRESTA RUN

KULM HOTEL

The ultra-luxurious, 'six-star' Kulm opened as St Moritz's first hotel over 150 years ago. It has a refined elegance and an aura of history and tradition to go with its comprehensive range of facilities. The Kulm is closely connected with the Cresta Club – the club secretary's office being located in the hotel.

CHARACTER Traditional luxury **ROOMS** 173 **FEATURES** 'Six-star' service; indoor pool with panoramic mountain views; gym; Jacuzzi; steam bath; salt grotto; infrared cubicle; caldariums and saunas; thalasso-therapy treatments; massages; ice-skating rink; curling; walking distance from Corviglia ski lift; sun terrace; four restaurants; two bars (including the Sunny Bar, which serves sushi and is decorated with Cresta Run memorabilia); concierge **LOCATION** Next to the Cresta Run

TAKE ME THERE

thebigshortbreak.co.uk
+44 (0)20 7978 7333

P.S. THE BEST WAY TO
NEGOTIATE SHUTTLECOCK
CORNER IS TO AIM FOR THE
BROOMSTICK AS YOU ENTER
THE TURN. FOR THOSE WHO
MISJUDGE IT, STRAW IS LAID OUT
TO CUSHION YOUR LANDING.

EXPERIENCE THIS »

AN OVERNIGHT CRUISE ON A PRIVATE DHOW IS A GREAT WAY TO EXPLORE THE COASTLINE OF OMAN. DOLPHINS OFTEN SWIM ALONGSIDE, AND YOU CAN JUMP OVERBOARD FOR A SWIM. THE MOONLIGHT ON THE WATER AND THE VIEWS OF THE RUGGED HAJAR MOUNTAINS AT DAWN ARE BEAUTIFUL.

MUST SEE The beautiful Sultan Qaboos Grand Mosque in Muscat – a modern architectural masterpiece » The fjords and fishing villages of the Musandam Peninsula » Turtles, rays and colourful corals on a snorkelling or diving trip to the Damaniyat Islands (near Muscat) or at Musandam MUST DO Paraglide into the Evason Hideaway at Zighy Bay – a unique way to arrive at your hotel » Discover the traditional way to climb a date palm tree » Learn a few words of Arabic RESTAURANTS/ BARS The restaurant at the Chedi in Muscat is one of Oman's best SOUVENIRS Gold and silver jewellery from the Muttrah souq in Muscat » Frankincense and a clay incense burner BOOK TO PACK The Road to Ubar: Finding the Atlantis of the Sands by Nicholas Clapp DON'T FORGET… Your mask and snorkel (but if you do, they can be provided) PRICE ■ ■ ■ □ □

BEST FOR… WINTER SUN » In contrast to its glitzy neighbour the United Arab Emirates, where the fast-forward dash for the future dominates all, the Sultanate of Oman remains a much more traditional place. That is not to say that the modern world has not arrived in Oman, but the pace of change has been much more carefully managed, with the happy result that the country remains one of the most unspoilt in the Middle East. To be fair, Oman has natural advantages over the Gulf states, which have had to rely to an extent on manufacturing artificial tourist attractions. Blessed with spectacular mountain, desert and coastal scenery, it enjoys a calm, relaxed atmosphere instead of a frenzy of construction. A handful of top-class beach hotels in the vicinity of the capital, Muscat, and in Musandam – an exclave that juts into the Straits of Hormuz at the tip of the Arabian Peninsula – make ideal destinations for some winter sun within reasonable flying time of the UK. Chill out in the shade of a palm tree and enjoy spa treatments, snorkelling or peaceful dhow trips along the coast. For something a little more active there are watersports, including some excellent diving, while the dramatic fjord-like scenery of Musandam and the untouched landscapes of the interior are also well worth exploring.

TAKE ME THERE
thebigshortbreak.co.uk
+44 (0)20 7978 7333

ARABIAN ESCAPE

7.5 HRS FROM UK TO MUSCAT
7 HRS FROM UK TO DUBAI

1 DAYS
2 DAYS OFF WORK

DEC 19°/27° JAN 17°/25° FEB 18°/26°

DAY 1 Arrive early morning into Muscat after overnight flight (or Dubai for Zighy Bay) » Private transfer to hotel » Day to relax on the beach, swim and enjoy watersports or spa treatments » Dine on the beach, under the stars

DAY 2 Day at leisure, with possible activities including dhow trips, fishing, diving, snorkelling and visits to the local souqs » Evening cruise on a traditional dhow with sundowner drinks

DAY 3 As per Day 2, or take a boat trip to a secluded bay for a private picnic, visit local fishing villages, relax with a good book or have your hands or feet hennaed in traditional Arabian style

DAY 4 Morning at leisure before transfer back to the airport for return flight home, arriving early evening

ARABIAN
ESCAPE

THE CHEDI, MUSCAT
A stylish beachfront hotel with
a chic, minimalist design, overlooking
the warm waters of the Gulf of Oman.
*(Opening pages; previous page; this
page, top and bottom)*

CHARACTER Luxury beach hotel
ROOMS 151 **FEATURES** Rooms and
private villas with ocean or mountain
views; 350-metre private sandy beach;
gardens; two swimming pools (one
for kids, one for adults); spa; two
tennis courts; gym; poolside bar;
excellent restaurant; diving; dhow
trips **LOCATION** Just outside Muscat

EVASON HIDEAWAY & SPA
AT ZIGHY BAY
A five-star beach resort set on
a private bay on Oman's remote
northern coast. Probably the only
hotel in the world where you have
the option to arrive by paraglider.
(Far page, bottom left)

CHARACTER Luxury beach resort
ROOMS 82 pool villas **FEATURES**
Mile-long sandy beach; private marina;
watersports including diving; spa; three
restaurants and poolside deli; two bars;
beach volleyball; gym; yoga; Pilates;
game fishing (on a catch and release
basis); dhow trips; wide variety of other
activities and excursions **LOCATION**
Musandam Peninsula

ADDITIONAL ACCOMMODATION
AL BUSTAN PALACE (MUSCAT)
BARR AL JISSAH RESORT (MUSCAT)

TAKE ME THERE
thebigshortbreak.co.uk
+44 (0)20 7978 7333

PS MAKE SURE YOU
DO YOUR SUMS CORRECTLY
WHEN HAGGLING IN MUSCAT'S
SOUQS – THE OMANI RIAL IS
ONE OF THE FEW CURRENCIES
IN THE WORLD THAT IS WORTH
MORE THAN THE POUND.

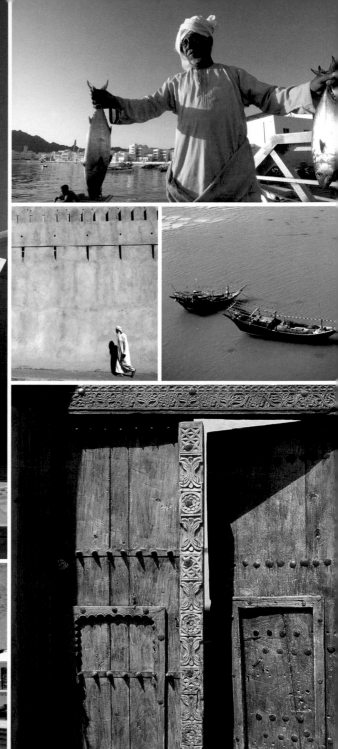

EXPERIENCE THIS »

WITNESS WHAT THE LOCALS CALL *ENROSADIRA* – THE EFFECT AT SUNSET WHEN THE PALE LIMESTONE CLIFF-FACES OF THE DOLOMITES GLOW A DOZEN DIFFERENT SHADES OF PINK, RED AND GOLD. THE VALPAROLA PASS IS A GREAT PLACE FROM WHICH TO WATCH THIS NATURAL LIGHT-SHOW.

ITALY

San Cassiano

Venice

MUST SEE Spectacular mountain scenery » First World War fortifications on the Col di Lana and Mt Lagazuoi. The Dolomites were the scene of high-altitude trench warfare » The parading *fashionistas* in Cortina d'Ampezzo MUST DO Ski the 'Sella Ronda' – the 24-mile circular route around the Sella massif » Eat Ladin specialities such as *panicia* (a special barley soup) » Have a massage using oil made from arnica plants, hand-picked in the alpine meadows every July RESTAURANTS/BARS St Hubertus restaurant at the Rosa Alpina has two Michelin stars (+39 0471 849 500) SOUVENIRS A copy of the cookbook *St Hubertus and the flavour of the Dolomites* by the chef at the Rosa Alpina BOOK TO PACK *The Name of the Rose* by Umberto Eco DON'T FORGET… Your *gioia di vivere* PRICE ■ □ □ □ □

BEST FOR… THE HIGH LIFE » For cognoscenti of such things, the Dolomites, a south-eastern range of the Alps, are considered to be amongst the most beautiful mountains in the world. Rising up from the snowfields and forests below, their dramatic, ragged peaks are particularly spectacular at dawn and sunset. One cluster of mountains known as the Cinque Torri was a source of inspiration for Tolkien when writing *The Lord of the Rings*. At the heart of the Dolomites is the Alta Badia region, which lies on the cultural border between Italy and the German-speaking Tyrol (though many of the locals still speak Ladin – an ancient language with Latin roots that has survived in the mountain valleys). The regional cuisine reflects these various influences, and the area has the highest concentration of Michelin-starred restaurants in the Alps. There is no better place from which to explore this enticing region than the village of San Cassiano and the Hotel Rosa Alpina, owned and managed for three generations by the Pizzinini family, who built the first ski-lift in San Cassiano back in the 1950's. Here, guests can enjoy outstanding food and wine, a renowned spa, and direct access to the vast 'Dolomiti Superski' domain. There is a word for this: 'civilised'.

TAKE ME THERE
thebigshortbreak.co.uk
+44 (0)20 7978 7333

SKI THE DOLOMITES

✈ 2.5 HRS FROM UK

🧳 4 DAYS
2 DAYS OFF WORK

☀ DEC -5°/6°; JAN -6°/5°
FEB -4°/7°

DAY 1 Fly to Venice and drive (or be driven) to San Cassiano, stopping at one of the mountain viewpoints to admire the scenery » Settle in at the Rosa Alpina and have supper at the 'Fondue Stube'

DAY 2 Full day's skiing on the expansive pistes of the Dolomiti Superski region » Alternatively, take a mountain guide and go snowshoeing or cross-country skiing in the forests (keep an eye out for chamois) » Sauna or spa treatment » Supper at the Rosa Alpina's gourmet 'St Hubertus' restaurant

DAY 3 Spend the day skiing the Sella Ronda or the Marmolada Glacier, or go on the Santa Croce ski tour – a panoramic-gastronomic ski tour of Alta Badia, eating at small mountain refuges which serve excellent food » Alternatively, go shopping in nearby Cortina d'Ampezzo

DAY 4 Time for more skiing or spa treatments in the morning before transfer back to Venice for return flight home

SKI THE
DOLOMITES

HOTEL ROSA ALPINA

One of the finest hotels in the Alps, the family-owned-and-run Rosa Alpina is set in the small village of San Cassiano at the heart of the Dolomites, not far from Cortina d'Ampezzo. *(Previous page; this page, bottom; far page, top left)*

CHARACTER Alpine lodge **ROOMS** 51 **FEATURES** Easy access to the ski slopes; provision of ski passes, instructors and mountain guides; Daniela Steiner spa; indoor pool; sauna; steambath; sun terrace; gym; three restaurants (including the Michelin-starred St Hubertus); wine bar; log fires; babysitting service **LOCATION** San Cassiano

TAKE ME THERE

thebigshortbreak.co.uk
+44 (0)20 7978 7333

PS A 'DOLOMITI SUPERSKI' PASS OFFERS UNRESTRICTED ACCESS TO THE LARGEST SKI NETWORK IN THE WORLD: 460 LIFTS AND 760 MILES OF SLOPES IN TOTAL. MORE THAN ENOUGH FOR A BIG SHORT BREAK.

EXPERIENCE THIS »

GO ICE FISHING OFF THE COAST OF MUHU ISLAND. THE CHEF AT PÄDASTE MANOR WILL PREPARE YOUR FRESH CATCH FOR BREAKFAST, COOKED IN A CRUST OF SEA SALT AND SERVED WITH CHILLED VODKA.

AT A GLANCE

TALLINN &
MUHU ISLAND

ESTONIA

Tallinn

Muhu Island

MUST SEE The spire of St Olav's Church that dominates the Tallinn skyline — once the tallest building in Europe and later used by the KGB to send radio transmissions » Tallinn's gothic Town Hall » Sunset over the ice-bound Baltic

MUST DO Walk the city walls of Old Tallinn » Go snowshoeing through frozen winter landscapes on Muhu Island » Try a 'Muhu hay bath' or a 'Scandinavian salt body scrub' at the Pädaste Manor spa **RESTAURANTS/BARS**

Olde Hansa — the best of the many medieval-themed restaurants — touristy but atmospheric (Vana turg 1, + 372 627 9020) **SOUVENIRS** Something from the Christmas market in Tallinn or a traditional embroidered woollen

blanket from Muhu Island **BOOK TO PACK** *Treading Air* by Jaan Kross **DON'T FORGET...** Your Estonian phrase book — the language is considered one of the hardest in the world **PRICE** ■■□□□

BEST FOR… A ROMANTIC WINTER ESCAPE » Once a key member of the Hanseatic League — a network of mercantile city-states that controlled trade in the Baltic — Tallinn used its resulting wealth to create what is today the best-preserved medieval town in northern Europe. The winding, cobbled streets of its compact, picture-postcard Old Town — still largely encircled by the original city walls — are lined with former guild halls, warehouses and merchants' homes, while the walls themselves are interspersed with towers of various shapes and sizes that have earthy names such as Tall Hermann, Fat Margaret and *Kiek in de Kök* (really). With a dusting of snow in winter, it all looks particularly beautiful. Long subject to Moscow, Tallinn also has Tsarist and Soviet heritage to explore, but to see a completely different side of Estonia, head for the rural tranquillity of Muhu Island in the Baltic. Here you can find unspoilt nature, sleepy farming and fishing villages, and Estonia's top spa-hotel. Go snowshoeing through peaceful winter landscapes, looking for elk and boar, take horse-drawn sledge rides through forests of juniper, pine and birch, and enjoy innovative local cuisine by a cosy fireplace. Alternatively, just unwind with a spa treatment or two and enjoy the seclusion.

TAKE ME THERE
thebigshortbreak.co.uk
+44 (0)20 7978 7333

TALLINN & MUHU ISLAND

✈ 3 HRS FROM UK

🧳 5 DAYS
3 DAYS OFF WORK

☀ DEC -7°/-1°; JAN -10°/-4°
FEB -11°/-4°

DAY 1 Morning flight to Tallinn and transfer to the Three Sisters hotel » Afternoon to explore the Old Town — a UNESCO World Heritage Site — and go shopping at the Christmas market » Evening to sample Tallinn's nightlife

DAY 2 Morning to explore more of Tallinn » Drive south-west to the coast » Short ferry ride to Muhu Island through the sea ice and continue to Pädaste Manor » Sunset walk on the seashore, followed by a glass of *vin chaud* around a bonfire

DAY 3 Day to relax and enjoy spa treatments, or explore the island: try fishing or snow-shoeing: go on a guided nature walk or a horse-drawn sled ride » Supper of elk carpaccio and roasted scallops, then watch a classic film in Pädaste's private cinema

DAY 4 Day to relax or explore more of the island: visit Koguva fishing village, the 13th-century fort-church of St Catherine's, or the Kaali meteorite crater on neighbouring Saaremaa Island » Evening soak in the outdoor hot tub

DAY 5 Morning at Pädaste Manor » Drive back to Tallinn for return flight home

TALLINN & MUHU ISLAND

THREE SISTERS

A stylish boutique hotel occupying three attractive medieval merchant houses on a cobbled street in the heart of Tallinn's old town. *(Far page, middle)*

CHARACTER Boutique design hotel **ROOMS** 23 **FEATURES** Good restaurant; library with fireplace; wine bar; masseur on call; easy walking distance to the city's main attractions **LOCATION** Central Tallinn

PÄDASTE MANOR

A small, luxurious spa-hotel set on an island in the Baltic Sea, just off the coast of Estonia. *(Previous page; this page, bottom)*

CHARACTER Seaside spa hotel **ROOMS** 14 **FEATURES** Historic building surrounded by landscaped parkland; spa with steam bath, wood-fired sauna and outdoor hot tub; horse-drawn sledge rides; snowshoeing; fishing; gourmet cuisine; good wine cellar; private cinema **LOCATION** Muhu Island

TAKE ME THERE

thebigshortbreak.co.uk
+44 (0)20 7978 7333

 WATCH THE SUN GO DOWN AND THE STARS COME UP FROM THE OUTDOOR, SEA-WATER HOT TUB OVERLOOKING THE BAY AT PÄDASTE, BUT KEEP YOUR HAT ON OR YOUR HAIR WILL FREEZE.

EXPERIENCE THIS »

BY THE TIME YOU REACH TURN THIRTEEN OF THE
LILLEHAMMER OLYMPIC BOBSLEIGH TRACK, YOU'LL
BE EXPERIENCING G-FORCE EQUIVALENT TO FLYING
A JET FIGHTER.

MUST SEE The faces of people who have just completed the bob run » The frozen lakes around Lillehammer from a snowmobile » Ski jumpers flying from the Olympic ski jump in Hafjell » The largest troll in the world at Hunderfossen **MUST DO** Ride the skeleton from the Senior Start » Ski the Olympic downhill course at Kvitfjell » Eat reindeer stew **RESTAURANTS/BARS** For après-bobsleigh, the Brenneriet Nightclub is the local favourite (Elvegata 19) **SOUVENIRS** A traditional Norwegian woolly hat with ear flaps » Reindeer skin slippers » A faster pulse **BOOK TO PACK** *Cool Runnings and Beyond: The Story of the Jamaica Bobsleigh Team* by Chris Stokes **DON'T FORGET…** Masking tape – for taping up the toe ends of your shoes when you ride the skeleton. This will stop them getting worn through as they touch the ice at 60mph **PRICE** ■ ■ ■ □ □

BEST FOR… WANNABE FIGHTER PILOTS » Usually the preserve of lycra-clad Olympians, mere mortals can also experience the thrill of bobsleighing by visiting the Olympic track just outside Lillehammer – the venue for the 1994 Winter Games. After a briefing and a walk of the course, don a crash helmet, climb aboard a four-man bobsleigh (steered by a professional pilot-cum-brakeman) and off you go. Rattling down the track on knife-edge blades, the bullet-shaped craft reaches speeds of up to 80mph and generates forces of 5G around the fastest bends. Like all adrenalin sports it's scary, but as soon as you've done it once you'll want to do it again. In the unlikely event that the bob is not enough of a rush for you, try a solo, head-first descent on a 'skeleton'; unlike the Cresta Run in Switzerland, which only men are allowed to ride, the liberal Norwegians even allow women to have a go. The Lillehammer area offers plenty of other winter sports to fill your remaining time, from ice climbing and snowmobile safaris to skiing the Olympic runs at Hafjell and Kvitfjell. For anyone feeling over-stimulated, a brief visit to the nearby Norwegian Road Museum should have the desired effect. You'll be relieved to hear there is 'ample parking space'.

TAKE ME THERE
thebigshortbreak.co.uk
+44 (0)20 7978 7333

BOBSLEIGH IN NORWAY

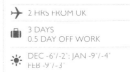

✈ 2 HRS FROM UK

🧳 3 DAYS
0.5 DAY OFF WORK

☀ DEC -6°/-2°; JAN -9°/-4°
FEB -9°/-3°

DAY 1 Afternoon flight to Oslo » Catch the train to Lillehammer » After supper, a full briefing on the days ahead should calm the nerves » Overnight at Hotel GudbrandsGard or Hunderfossen

DAY 2 Early start and transfer to the Olympic bobsleigh track » Safety briefing and walk the track » Ride the bob raft, followed by the real thing » Afternoon for skeleton racing

DAY 3 Morning for skiing, a skidoo safari in the hills or other winter activities » Lunch in a traditional *lavvo* (teepee-like) tent » Transfer back to Oslo for return flight home

BOBSLEIGH
IN NORWAY

QUALITY HOTEL & RESORT
HUNDERFOSSEN

For those with a keen interest in trolls, this is the quality place to stay, having a troll-themed restaurant and being close to an amusement park full of trolls. (It is also walking distance to the Olympic bob and luge track.)

CHARACTER Norwegian **ROOMS** 40 + 60 cabins in the grounds **FEATURES** Two restaurants (one troll-themed, one not); bar; saunas; solarium; gym **LOCATION** Hunderfossen

GUDBRANDSGARD HOTEL

One of Norway's best alpine hotels, set on the slopes at Kvitfjell – the country's most exclusive ski resort and site of the men's downhill for the 1994 Olympic Games.

CHARACTER Ski hotel **ROOMS** 85 **FEATURES** Indoor swimming pool; sauna; hot tub; gym; large outdoor terrace with mountain views; ski rental shop; direct access to the slopes; good restaurant; bar; nightclub **LOCATION** Kvitfjell

TAKE ME THERE
thebigshortbreak.co.uk
+44 (0)20 7978 7333

START
LILLEHAMMER

PS TAKE THE BACK SEAT
IN THE FOUR-MAN BOBSLEIGH
IF YOU WANT THE MOST
EXHILARATING RIDE. EVERY
MOVEMENT IS EXAGGERATED –
LIKE BEING AT THE BACK OF A
PLANE, BUT MUCH MORE FUN.

EXPERIENCE THIS »

THE MIGRATION SOUTH FROM THE MASAI MARA BEGINS
AROUND NOVEMBER, AND BY FEBRUARY THE PLAINS OF
THE SERENGETI ARE THE FEEDING GROUNDS FOR OVER
TWO MILLION WILDEBEEST, ZEBRA AND GAZELLE, CLOSELY
PURSUED BY THE INEVITABLE PREDATORS.

TANZANIA

Serengeti

Selous

MUST SEE The great migration in the Serengeti » An eagle riding the thermals in an African sky » The view from the rim of the Ngorongoro Crater » For history buffs, Tanzania was the scene of a little-known campaign between the British and the Germans during World War I. Trenches can still be seen in the Selous MUST DO An early morning walking safari in the Serengeti with expert Masai guides » A boat safari on Lake Tagalala in the Selous » Savour the liberating sense of space in the Serengeti RESTAURANTS/BARS n/a SOUVENIRS Masai *shuka* (blanket) » Tanzanian coffee, grown in the highlands around Mt Kilimanjaro » Avoid buying any souvenirs made from endangered animal parts BOOK TO PACK *An Ice-Cream War* by William Boyd DON'T FORGET... A field guide to the wildlife of East Africa PRICE ■ ■ ■ ■ ■

BEST FOR… CLASSIC SAFARI » Tanzania is home to two of Africa's most renowned game reserves: the legendary Serengeti in the north, and the sprawling Selous in the south. In the Masai language Serengeti means 'endless plains', and from the air it can appear like an ocean of grass. Stretching to the Kenyan border, where it merges with the Masai Mara, this is classic savannah scenery, and the setting for the great migration – one of the natural wonders of the world. Nearby is the remarkable Ngorongoro Crater, a huge volcanic caldera that serves as a natural enclosure for an incredible concentration of wildlife. The Serengeti may be big, but is still dwarfed by the Selous. Named after the famous hunter, it is now Africa's biggest wildlife sanctuary, comfortably larger than Switzerland. In contrast to the open plains of the Serengeti, the Selous is a wilderness of tangled jungle, characterised by thick clumps of monkey-filled palm trees and meandering 'sand rivers' that only flow in the wet season. Between them, these parks offer outstanding wildlife viewing, from free-roaming plains game to wallowing pods of hippo and rich bird life. The Selous is also one of the last refuges of the black rhino and the African wild dog.

TAKE ME THERE
thebigshortbreak.co.uk
+44 (0)20 7978 7333

**TANZANIA:
SERENGETI & SELOUS**

✈ 9.5 HRS FROM UK
2 HRS TO SERENGETI/
1 HR TO SELOUS

🧳 5 DAYS
3 DAYS OFF WORK

☀ DEC 18°/31°; JAN 18°/29°
FEB 18°/29°

DAY 1 Arrive in Dar es Salaam after an overnight flight, and connect by light aircraft to the Serengeti or Selous » Afternoon to relax » Evening game drive and sundowner drinks » Overnight at Nduara Loliondo or Beho Beho

DAY 2 Early start for a morning game drive with the Masai in the Serengeti, or in the Selous » Afternoon siesta » Evening game drive » Supper and drinks round the campfire

DAY 3 Morning game drive, or a boat safari in the Selous, with swimming in natural hot springs » Afternoon to relax » Further game viewing in the evening, followed by candlelit dinner under the stars

DAY 4 Morning game viewing » Afternoon to relax » Night drive to see nocturnal game, or camping out in the African bush

DAY 5 Final game drive in the early morning » Transfer to airstrip for return flights home

TANZANIA:
SERENGETI & SELOUS

NDUARA LOLIONDO
One of the most original safari camps in Africa, Nduara Loliondo is a mobile 'yurt camp' on the eastern edge of the Serengeti. *(Previous page)*

CHARACTER Mobile safari camp **ROOMS** 6 **FEATURES** Yurt-style tents; private guide and 4WD vehicle for each set of guests; expertly guided walking safaris with the Masai; night drives; traditional safari-style bucket showers; campfires in the evenings **LOCATION** Loliondo Masai concession area

BEHO BEHO
Set in the hills in the northern part of the Selous Reserve, Beho Beho makes a luxurious base from which to explore one of Africa's greatest nature reserves. *(Far page, top left)*

CHARACTER Safari camp **ROOMS** 8 **FEATURES** Expertly guided walking safaris; game drives by open 4WD; boat safaris on nearby Lake Tagalala; swimming in natural hot springs; bar; billiards table; swimming pool; panoramic views over the Rufiji River flood plain **LOCATION** Selous Game Reserve

ADDITIONAL ACCOMMODATION
SERENGETI SAFARI CAMP (SERENGETI)
SAND RIVERS (SELOUS)

TAKE ME THERE
thebigshortbreak.co.uk
+44 (0)20 7978 7333

PS TO AVOID BORING YOUR FRIENDS AND RELATIVES WITH 'DISTANT SPECK ON THE HORIZON' WILDLIFE PICTURES, IT IS WELL WORTH INVESTING IN A CAMERA WITH A DECENT TELEPHOTO LENS.

EXPERIENCE THIS »
FOR A FUN FAMILY OUTING, TAKE A HORSE-DRAWN SLEIGH FROM THE COVERED BRIDGE IN LECH TO THE PRETTY LITTLE HAMLET OF ZUG FOR A TRADITIONAL FONDUE SUPPER.

MUST SEE The deer being fed in the Engerle Forest » Spectacular alpine scenery on the 'White Ring' ski tour » The little 'uns showing off their new skills in the weekly ski race **MUST DO** Glide through winter landscapes on a horse-drawn sleigh ride » Have a hot chocolate on the terrace of a mountain restaurant » Ride the floodlit, mile-long toboggan run from Oberlech to Lech **RESTAURANTS/BARS** Located in the car-free village of Oberlech, the Alter Goldener Berg serves excellent alpine fare in a cosy atmosphere. Accessed via cable-car from Lech (+43 5583 22 050) **SOUVENIRS** Knitted scarves » Felt slippers » Traditional Christmas tree decorations **BOOK TO PACK** *There and Then: The Travel Writing of James Salter* by James Salter (adults) » *Heidi* by Johanna Spyri (kids) **DON'T FORGET...** Your snowball-making skills **PRICE** ■ ■ ■ □ □

BEST FOR… FUTURE SKI CHAMPS » It's always a bit galling when you're skiing along in what you think is quite an accomplished style, only to be overtaken by a stream of youngsters wearing crash-helmets, fearlessly bombing down the pistes like colourful cannonballs. At least if they were *your* children, you could take pride in the precocious little nippers. This is where Austria's renowned ski schools come in, and Lech has one of the most highly respected of all. A picturesque Tyrolean village with an onion-domed church, horse-drawn sleighs and a wooden bridge across the river, Lech has managed to retain much of its old-world charm and is the perfect family resort. With expert tuition from the ski school's highly qualified instructors, your kids will soon be progressing from snowplough to parallel turns and schussing. For the youngest, there's also an on-slope kindergarten where they can play and get their first taste of skiing, leaving parents to enjoy the extensive pistes of the Arlberg area, including the famous 'White Ring' ski tour to nearby Zürs. Besides skiing, Lech offers plenty of other options for keeping young minds entertained, from ice-skating and a flood-lit toboggan run, to a traditional Christmas market or watching deer being fed in the forests.

TAKE ME THERE
thebigshortbreak.co.uk
+44 (0)20 7978 7333

LECH: OLD SCHOOL
MEETS SKI SCHOOL

✈ 2 HRS FROM UK

🧳 5 DAYS
3 DAYS OFF WORK

☀ DEC -6°/0°; JAN -8°/-1°
FEB -7°/2°

DAY 1 Fly to Innsbruck and transfer to Lech » Check in at the Hotel Kristiania (your lift passes will be waiting for you at reception) » Collect pre-arranged ski hire » Supper and overnight at the Kristiania

DAYS 2-4 Children spend days at ski school or with a private instructor » Adults free to enjoy the excellent skiing of the Arlberg area » Family lunches on the mountain » Afternoons for more skiing or alternative winter activities such as ice-skating and snowshoeing » Relaxing foot massages for parents at the Kristiania

DAY 5 Morning to ski, with lunch in a mountain restaurant » Afternoon transfer back to Innsbruck for return flight home

LECH: OLD SCHOOL
MEETS SKI SCHOOL

HOTEL KRISTIANIA

A small, chalet-style ski hotel
in the picturesque village of Lech,
the family-run Kristiania offers
top class accommodation and
a homely, low-key atmosphere.
(This page, bottom)

CHARACTER Luxury ski chalet
ROOMS 30 **FEATURES** Restaurant
serving excellent Austrian cuisine;
well-stocked cellar; sun terrace;
sauna; in-room spa treatments
and massages; cosy bar; log fires;
concierge; child-care service; pets
welcome **LOCATION** Lech

TAKE ME THERE

thebigshortbreak.co.uk
+44 (0)20 7978 7333

P3 DON'T BE BAD PARENTS: REMEMBER TO BOOK SKI SCHOOL OR PRIVATE INSTRUCTORS WELL AHEAD, AS THE RESORT IS ALWAYS BUSY DURING SCHOOL HOLIDAYS AND HALF TERMS.

WHO CAN 'TAKE YOU THERE'? » Each Big Short Break in this book concludes with the words 'take me there'. To experience these trips for real, contact us at Original Travel — an award-winning travel company specialising in bespoke Big Short Breaks since 2002.

We are a team of passionate travellers who have lived, worked and travelled in over 120 countries. With first-hand knowledge of every destination in this book (several of us make cameo appearances in the photos) we have the inside track on what is best to see and do in the limited time available — after all, on a short break there's no time for trial and error.

When you travel with us, we take care of everything from flights to activities and everything in between, and offer one point of contact (with a real human being) throughout the booking process. Since our launch, we have sent thousands of clients to an array of inspiring destinations across the globe, and are delighted to report that an ever-increasing number of them have gone on to become serial 'Big Short Breakers'.

To tailor-make your ideal Big Short Break, call us on +44 (0)20 7978 7333 or email us at info@thebigshortbreak.co.uk

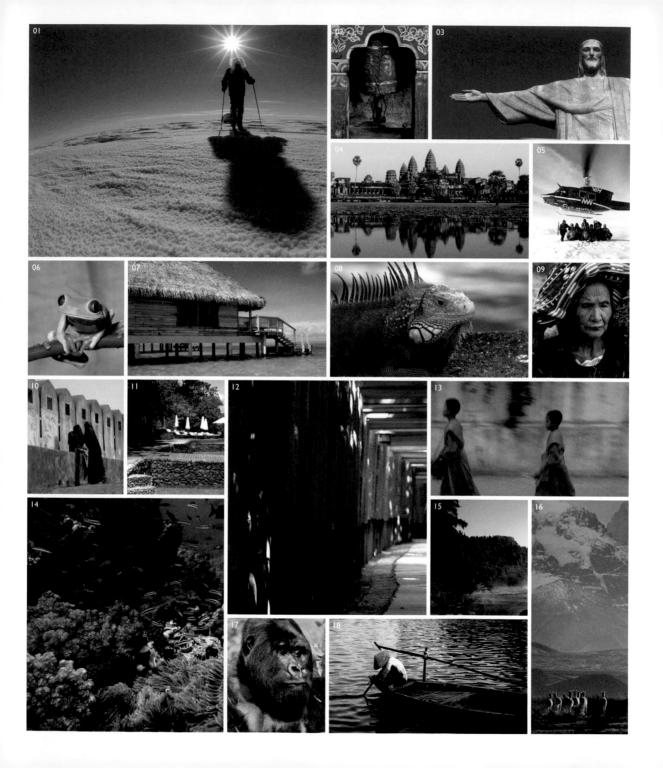

BEYOND THE BIG SHORT BREAK » If you like the look of our Big Short Breaks, and have a little extra time to play with, why not try something even bigger? 'Beyond the Big Short Break' is a portfolio of our favourite long-haul destinations, from Patagonia to Polynesia. As with our Big Short Breaks, these longer-haul trips cover a broad spectrum, so whether it's a desert island, a cultural journey or an adventurous challenge you're after (or a combination of all these) we hope you will find it in the big 'Beyond'. And if you're not sure where to go, hopefully the appetisers opposite will provide some *haute cuisine* for thought…

TAKE ME THERE
beyondthebigshortbreak.co.uk
+44 (0)20 7978 7333

DESTINATIONS

01 ANTARCTICA	09 GUATEMALA	17 UGANDA
02 BHUTAN	10 INDIA	18 VIETNAM
03 BRAZIL	11 INDONESIA	& many more besides…
04 CAMBODIA	12 JAPAN	
05 CANADA	13 LAOS	
06 COSTA RICA	14 MALDIVES	
07 FRENCH POLYNESIA	15 NEW ZEALAND	
08 GALAPAGOS ISLANDS	16 PATAGONIA	

A HUGE THANK YOU TO » The team at Original Travel, and particularly Emily Morris; the team at Inaria, and particularly Debora Berardi, Andrew Thomas, Anna Leaver, Georgie Stephens, and Georgie Melsom; Mike Sage at CTD; Hugh Brune at Portfolio; Matt Hyslop, Paul Fournel and James Fletcher

PHOTOGRAPHY » Special thanks to the following for their photographic contributions: Achim Mende, Ain Avik, Alan Keohane, Alastair Poulain, Amanda Edwards, Andrew Thomas, Andy Bain, Anette Kellerman, Anna Perry, Arabella Arbuthnott, Austrian National Tourist Office, Ben Forbes, Benguerra Lodge, Birkenhead House, Bjorn Thunaes, Camilla Stoddart, Carmen Derosas, Cees Van Roeden, Chamonix Tourist Board (M Colonel, F E Cormier, Pascal Tournaire, Tutt-Pyk), Charlotte Asprey, Chris Simpson, Christian Alsing, Christian Perret, Christophe Migeon, Croatian National Tourist Office, Dan Scott, Dana Allen, Debora Berardi, Dorte Krogh, Ed Judd, Ed Reeves, Elsa's Kopje, Emily Morris, Emirates Al Maha Desert Resort & Spa, Emma Badenoch, Erlend Folstad, Esben Haakenstad, Frode Jenssen, Getty Images/Michael & Patricia Fogden, Getty Images/ Stockbyte, Hayley Poulain, Henry Trygg, Hotel Pitrizza, James Fletcher, Jason LaFrenais, J-M Del Moral, Jo Vincent, John Davis, John Warburton-Lee, Jordanian Tourist Board, Jørn Henriksen, Jukkasjärvi Vildmarks Turer, Jumeirah Bab Al Shams Desert Resort, Lars Burell, Lech Zürs Tourismus GmbH, Loisaba, Madeira Tourist Board, Malta Tourism Authority, Marcel Jolibois, Marianne Springel, Matt Hyslop, Mike Skinner, Mike Wiegele Heliskiing, Nick Newbury, Nicolaj Perjesi, Nicolas Tosi, Nigel Dennis, Nigel Pavitt, Nina Bailey, Nomad Tanzania, Oman Tourism Office UK & IRE, Österreich Werbung/Wiesenhafer, P Carrier, Paul Fournel, Paul Joynson-Hicks, Per Kristiansen, Peter Rosén, Ragnar Hartvig, Raoul Crettenand, Richard Ryan, Riksgränsen Hotel, Robin Pope Safaris, Rod Haestier, Ronald Asprey, Rosie Barclay, Rosie Kennedy, Royal Malewane, Ryan Larraman, St Moritz Tourist Board, Shangri-La's Barr Al Jissah Resort, Skiclub Arlberg, Solvin Zankl, South African Tourism, Spitsbergen Travel, Stephan Brückner, Synnøve Haga, SYS The Ultimate Event Company, Tallinn City Tourist Office & Convention Bureau, Teddy Wakefield, Tenerife Tourism Corporation, Thanos Hotels, Theodore Kristensen, Tom Barber, Tommy Simonsen, Toomas Volmer, Turespãna, Tysfjord Turistsenter, Virgin Limited Edition, VisitDenmark, VisitSweden (imagebank.sweden.se), white-desert.com, Wilderness Safaris, William Abranowicz and Zelkjo Kelemen

MEMBERSHIP » Congratulations on purchasing this book – you have demonstrated impeccable judgement (and if you received it as a gift, well done for having such discerning friends or relatives). As a reward, Original Travel has prepared some special treats for you. On the card below you will find a unique number, which you can use to activate your membership via the website **thebigshortbreak.co.uk.*** Once registered…

» We will refund £20 off your first Big Short Break booking (i.e. you get the cost of the book back).

» Each time you book one of the featured 52 Big Short Breaks you will receive an additional free goodie, exclusive to members, ranging from spa treatments to ski hire or a desert camel ride. Details of the specific perks for each trip can be seen on the relevant trip page of the website.

» We will email you our monthly newsletter so that you'll be the first to hear about special offers, travel updates and any new Big Short Breaks.

Those are the carrots. There is no stick.

Your Big Short Break membership card should be here. If it's been pilfered, you can activate your membership by calling us on: +44 (0)20 7978 7333

* If for any reason you can't get online (or don't do computers) just write to us with your membership number and personal details at: Original Travel, 1B The Village, 101 Amies Street, London SW11 2JW …and we'll do the rest for you.